MAKE IT, TAKE IT

MAKE IT, TAKE IT

16 CUTE and CLEVER Projects to Sew with Friends

Krista Hennebury

Martingale®
Create with Confidence

Make It, Take It
16 Cute and Clever Projects to Sew with Friends
© 2015 by Krista Hennebury

Martingale®
19021 120th Ave. NE, Ste. 102
Bothell, WA 98011-9511 USA
ShopMartingale.com

Printed in China
20 19 18 17 16 15   8 7 6 5 4 3 2 1

Library of Congress Cataloging-in-Publication Data is available upon request.

ISBN: 978-1-60468-487-2

CREDITS

PUBLISHER AND CHIEF VISIONARY OFFICER: Jennifer Erbe Keltner

EDITOR IN CHIEF: Mary V. Green

DESIGN DIRECTOR: Paula Schlosser

MANAGING EDITOR: Karen Costello Soltys

ACQUISITIONS EDITOR: Karen M. Burns

TECHNICAL EDITOR: Nancy Mahoney

COPY EDITOR: Sheila Chapman Ryan

PRODUCTION MANAGER: Regina Girard

COVER AND INTERIOR DESIGNER: Adrienne Smitke

PHOTOGRAPHER: Brent Kane

ILLUSTRATOR: Christine Erikson

- -

Thanks to Drygoods Design in Seattle, Washington, for providing a beautiful location for photography.

- -

CONTENTS

house rules

- have fun
- get comfortable
- leave your workstation ready for its next use
- Return design boards + pin free
- be safe – watch your fingers with cutting tools + machines

thank you!

INTRODUCTION

While I love creating in my small home sewing room surrounded by colorful fabric, I have a lot more fun sewing on retreats surrounded by wonderful friends. Not long after I began quilting in 2000, a friend and I bravely signed up for an overnight retreat sponsored by a local quilt shop. We were the youngest participants and had no idea what to expect on that three-day weekend with much more experienced quilters. It was one of the first times away from my young children and the first time I'd had a sleepover with that many women since my first year in residence at university. I can honestly say that the entire weekend was a roaring success! So much so, that I've been on more than 50 retreats since then!

Before you start thinking that I've abandoned my family altogether, let me explain. Shortly after that first glorious weekend of sewing, sharing, learning, relaxing, and—some would say most importantly—eating food prepared by someone other than me, I started my own successful day-retreat business called Quilt by the Bay. I've been running this fully-catered, 13-hour day retreat for the past 10 years, welcoming both traditional and modern quilters to a brightly lit community hall that overlooks the ocean just north of Vancouver, Canada. The retreats are luxurious days spent away from work and family obligations, with plenty of room to spread out and sew with other like-minded people. All participants get their own six-foot-long banquet table. I supply ironing stations, raised basting and cutting tables, door prizes, goodie bags, and all of the food and drinks. Every retreat includes show-and-tell during afternoon tea.

> *More and more quilters are embracing the idea of traveling to sew with friends.*

In addition to the one-day retreats, I run a four-day retreat for 28 women every November in a wonderfully secluded mountain lodge (with no cell-phone reception!). I also like to get away a couple of times a year with small groups of four or five sewing friends. I've stayed in rented resort condos, summer homes at the lake, church

Left: "Ultimate Equipment Tote", page 12;
Right: "Knitwit Needle Clutch", page 40

If an overnight getaway isn't in the cards, why not plan an impromptu sewing day at home with friends or fellow guild members?

camps, retreat centers, and a tranquil island home. These weekends with friends are much more than a chance to tackle the lingering UFO pile. They are a shared experience of fellowship where we solve so much more than machine-tension issues: parenting, fitness, marriages, health problems, music, movies, recipes, favorite blogs, and online shops are all up for discussion. I always return home tired, but content. Inevitably, I'm completely "sewn out," but satisfied with my productivity no matter how much, or how little, I managed to accomplish.

More and more quilters are embracing the idea of traveling to sew with friends. In 2013, I went to London, England, for a retreat. Three contributors to this book have traveled from their homes in

Left: "Posy Pillow", page 66;
Right: Lone Star Circle Quilt, page 86

Alaska, Washington, and Manitoba to attend my November retreat. With this book, it was my desire to bring together a virtual retreat with some of my favorite sewing-blogger friends. I asked them to design projects that would help you and your sewing supplies *travel* to retreat—you'll find these projects in "Take Your Sew on the Road" (page 11). Anyone who has tried packing a 24"-long acrylic ruler will truly appreciate the epic "Ultimate Equipment Tote" (page 12), designed to get your rulers safely there and back with all corners intact. There's even a stylish clutch for knitters to tote their interchangeable circular needle set!

In the "Sew When You Get There" section (page 65), you'll find a wonderful selection of both modern- and traditional-inspired quilting projects to make while *on retreat*. Quilters with some experience will find that the "Posy Pillow" (page 66) or "Stepping Stone Table Runner" (page 72) are doable in a day, while "Lone Star Circle Quilt" (page 86), "Orange Grove Quilt" (page 92), or "*Macaron* Delight Quilt" (page 98) may require a weekend retreat or more to complete. If an overnight getaway isn't in the cards, why not plan an impromptu sewing day at home with friends or fellow guild members? "Rainbow 'Round the Cabin Quilt" (page 104) is a fun afternoon quilting activity for a group of six friends that would be a wonderful way to introduce quilting to a beginner. Everyone contributes fabric, and everyone goes home with a completed lap-sized quilt top.

Left: An assortment of projects on a sewing work table;
Right top: detail of "Rainbow 'Round the Cabin Quilt," page 104;
Right bottom: detail of "Orange Grove Quilt," page 92

These retreat weekends with friends are much more than a chance to tackle the lingering UFO pile.

In order to include as many projects as possible, *Make It, Take It* does not include general quiltmaking techniques; however, everything you need to know, from cutting fabric to finishing a quilt, can be found at www.ShopMartingale.com/HowtoQuilt. Project-specific tricks and tips are highlighted throughout this book, so sewists of every level should have all of the information they need to complete the projects.

I hope you'll find inspiration in these pages and have fun making the projects in *Make It, Take It,* either at home or on your next retreat! I would love to hear from you—contact me any time through my blog, poppyprintcreates.blogspot.com.

Happy quilting!

Krista

Ultimate Equipment Tote

FINISHED SIZE: 26½" x 19"

Designed and made by Berene Campbell featuring Bark & Branch fabric by Eloise Renouf for Cloud 9 Organics

Safely transport your acrylic rulers, an 18" x 24" cutting mat, books and patterns, or even quilt blocks to retreat in this epic equipment tote. The main tote opens to reveal a removable padded ruler folder with pockets you can custom-sew to accommodate your personal ruler collection. Two bonus sleeve pockets and a zipper pocket on the tote's exterior will hold rotary cutters, smaller rulers, marking tools, and other notions you'll want along on retreat.

MATERIALS

Yardage is based on 42"-wide fabric unless otherwise noted.

1⅓ yards of denim fabric for tote exterior
1⅓ yards of cloud print for tote lining and tote exterior pocket
1¼ yards of tree print for ruler-folder exterior and tote pocket
1 yard of leaf print for ruler-folder pockets
⅞ yard of blue solid for ruler-folder lining
⅓ yard of red solid for tote pocket linings
1 fat quarter of bird print for tote zipper pocket
30" x 50" piece of low-loft batting
1½ yards of heavyweight interfacing
3¼ yards of 1"-wide nylon webbing for straps
5" length of ¾"-wide Velcro
1 nylon zipper, 7" long
Sharp embroidery scissors
Fabric-glue stick
Clover Wonder Clips (optional)
Basting pins or basting spray

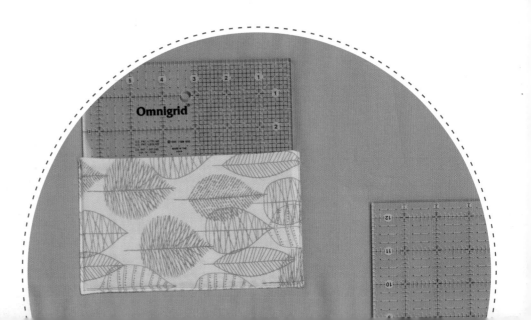

Project Notes

This project consists of two separate components, the cutting-mat tote and the removable ruler folder. Some fabrics are used for both items, as specified in the materials and cutting lists; however, you may use as many prints as you like. Refer to the cutting list, project photos, and illustrations for the placement of specific fabrics. All seam allowances are ¼" unless otherwise specified. For strength and durability, be sure to backstitch at the beginning and end of each seam.

CUTTING

All measurements include a ¼" seam allowance unless otherwise noted.

From the bird print, cut:
2 rectangles, 8½" x 11" (A)

From the red solid, cut:
1 rectangle, 8½" x 11" (A)
1 rectangle, 8" x 8½" (C)
1 rectangle, 8½" x 14" (E)

From the tree print, cut:
1 rectangle, 25" x 37½" (P)
1 rectangle, 7½" x 8½" (B)

From the cloud print, cut:
1 rectangle, 27" x 33" (J)
1 rectangle, 13" x 27" (K)
1 rectangle, 8½" x 13½" (D)

From the denim fabric, cut:
1 rectangle, 14" x 28" (I)
1 rectangle, 20" x 28" (H)
1 rectangle, 3½" x 8½" (F)
2 rectangles, 10¼" x 14" (G)

From the leaf print, cut:
1 rectangle, 25" x 28½" (L)
2 rectangles, 4½" x 7¼" (M)
2 rectangles, 4½" x 5½" (N)

From the blue solid, cut:
2 rectangles, 19" x 25" (O)

From the batting, cut:
1 rectangle, 30" x 35"
1 rectangle, 15" x 30"

From the heavyweight interfacing, cut:
2 rectangles, 18" x 24¼"

From the nylon webbing, cut:
2 pieces, 53" long

From the Velcro, cut:
2 pieces, 2" long

MAKING THE CUTTING-MAT TOTE

The lined tote has an exterior zippered pocket and exterior slot-style pockets for stowing extra sewing tools and notions.

Zipper Pocket

1. Place the bird-print A rectangles right sides together. Draw a ½" x 6" rectangle on the wrong side of one piece, 1¼" in from each side and 1¼" down from the top edge as shown. Draw a horizontal line across the middle of the rectangle, stopping ¼" from each end. Pin through both layers of fabric, above and below the drawn box.

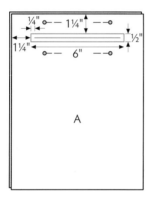

2. Using a very short stitch length, sew all the way around the marked box, pivoting with the needle down at each corner. With sharp embroidery scissors, cut through both layers of fabric along the marked center line, stopping ¼" from each end of the box. Snip diagonally into each corner of the box, taking care not to cut into the stitched line.

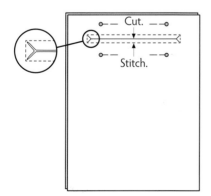

3. Push the top fabric through the slit so that the fabrics are now wrong sides together. Finger-press in place, gently tugging at the corners until the pieces are flat. Then press well with an iron. This creates a window opening for the zipper. Place the zipper under the window, making sure the metal stops are ½" beyond each end of the window so that you don't stitch over them and break a needle. Pin or glue the zipper in place. Using a zipper foot, topstitch all around the window as close to the edge as possible to secure the zipper and complete the zipper-pocket front.

Topstitch.

4. Place the red A rectangle right side up underneath the zipper-pocket front. Pin the three layers of fabric together. Baste ⅛" from the outer edges on all sides.

Slot Pockets

1. Place the tree-print B rectangle right sides together with the red C rectangle, aligning the top edges (the bottom edges will not be aligned). Stitch along the top edge. Press the seam allowances toward the red lining. Fold the red rectangle over the seam allowances to the wrong side of the tree-print rectangle to make a ¼" accent trim along the top of the pocket. Repeat the process using the cloud-print D rectangle and red E rectangle.

2. With both pockets right sides up, layer the B pocket on top of the D pocket, aligning the

bottom edges. Baste the pockets together using a ⅛" seam allowance along the side and bottom edges of the B pocket to complete the slot pocket unit.

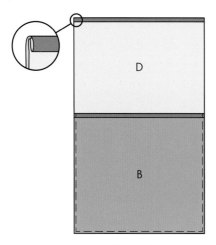

Slot pockets

Tote Exterior

1. With right sides together, sew the denim F rectangle to the top of the zipper pocket. Press the seam allowances toward the F rectangle. Topstitch along the seam on the F rectangle. Sew a denim G rectangle to each side of the zipper pocket. Press the seam allowances toward the G rectangles. Topstitch close to the seam on the G rectangles to make the bottom unit as shown in the diagram following step 4.

2. Aligning the 28" edges, pin the denim H rectangle to the bottom unit, right sides together. Sew the pieces together. Press the seam allowances open and topstitch along both sides of the seam to complete the F/G/H unit.

3. Pin or spray-baste the F/G/H unit to the 30" x 35" piece of batting. Similarly, baste the denim I rectangle to the 15" x 30" piece of batting. (Note that you will not have any backing fabric.) Quilt vertical lines 1" apart. *Do not to quilt over the zipper pocket.*

4. Center a piece of Velcro hooks on top of each piece F side seam, ¼" down from the top seam as shown. Topstitch the Velcro in place.

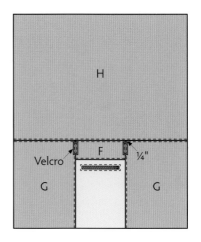

5. Trim the F/G/H unit as shown. Trim the cloud-print J rectangle in the same way. On the wrong side, mark a dot ¼" from the corner on both sides as indicated. Set aside the J rectangle. Trim the denim I rectangle to 13" x 27"

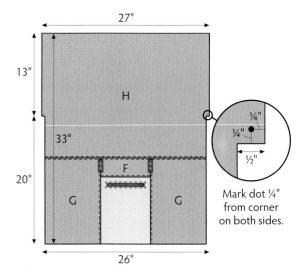

Mark dot ¼" from corner on both sides.

6. With the F/G/H unit right side up, position the slot pocket unit on top of the H rectangle, centering the pocket along the bottom edge of the unit as shown in the tote assembly diagram on page 17. Baste the pocket in place along the side and bottom edges.

7. To make the strap, center one end of a 53"-long piece of nylon webbing over the edges of

the pocket unit, raw edges aligned as shown in the tote assembly diagram. Pin the strap in place along one side of the pocket unit; then curve the strap back and down, centering it over the other side of the pocket. Make sure that the strap is not twisted at the handle end. Topstitch 1/16" from each side of the strap, pivoting and sewing across the top 1/4" below the main seam as shown.

8. Place the bottom edges of the I rectangle and the F/G/H unit adjacent to each other as shown in the tote assembly diagram. Using the strap position on the F/G/H unit as a guide, place the other strap on the I rectangle, aligning the ends of the strap with the edge of the rectangle. Pin the strap in place. Topstitch 1/16" from each side of the strap, pivoting and sewing across the strap 6" up from the bottom edge as shown.

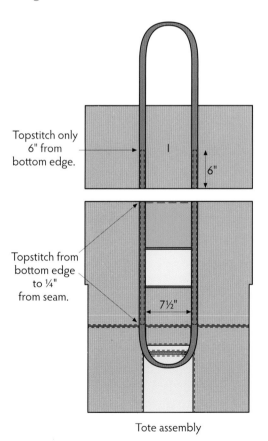

Topstitch only 6" from bottom edge.

Topstitch from bottom edge to 1/4" from seam.

Tote assembly

9. Place the F/G/H unit and the I rectangle right sides together, aligning the bottom edges

(the corresponding straps should be on top of each other). Pin (or use Wonder Clips) along the bottom edge to secure the layers. Sew the pieces together along the bottom edge, carefully backstitching over the straps. Press the seam allowances (including the strap ends) open. If desired, topstitch 1/8" along each side of the seam to secure the seam allowances open and prevent lumps in the bottom of the tote.

Tote Lining

1. Layer the cloud-print K rectangle right sides together with the denim I rectangle and align the long edges. Making sure the strap is out of the way, sew the pieces together along the long edge.

2. With right sides together, place the trimmed cloud-print J rectangle on top of the F/G/H unit, aligning the side cutouts and edges of the pieces as shown. Beginning and ending at the marked dots and stitching 1/4" from each outside edge, sew the pieces together.

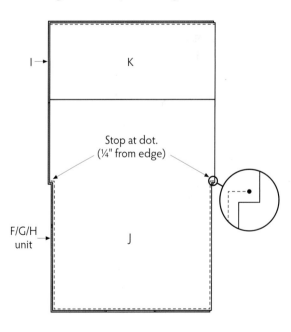

Stop at dot. (1/4" from edge)

3. Fold the I rectangle onto the F/G/H unit, right sides together along the seam between the pieces. Pin the sides together. Lift the K rectangle up, right sides together with the

J rectangle, and align the raw edges as shown. Pin the raw edges together. Note that the tote now resembles a T shape, with all of the side seams converging at the marked dots.

4. Sew down both sides of the I rectangle, stopping at the marked dots. Mark a 12" turning gap on the bottom edge of the K rectangle. Sew from each end of the gap along the bottom edge, then up the side edge to the marked dots. Trim the top corners of the J rectangle.

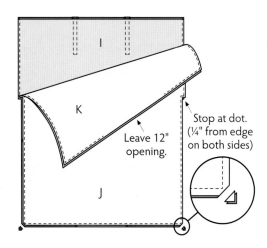

Bottom Gusset

1. Pinch one of the bottom corners of the denim I rectangle flat, placing the side seam on top of the bottom seam to form a triangle. Measure ½" from the corner and draw a 1" line perpendicular to the seam. Sew along the drawn line and trim away the corner fabric ¼" from the stitched line. Repeat the process on the other bottom corner of the denim I rectangle.

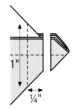

2. In the same way, make a gusset on the bottom corners of the cloud-print J rectangle.

Finishing

1. Turn the tote right side out through the 12" gap in the lining. Turn the seam allowance of the gap to the wrong side and press. Pin across the opening. Hand or machine sew the gap closed. Push the lining inside the tote.

2. Lay the tote on a flat surface with the flap closed. Lay the strap up over the flap, along the seams on either side of zippered pocket. Mark the position for the corresponding pieces of Velcro loops on the underside of the strap. Sew the Velcro in place on the strap. The Velcro will hold the strap up when the tote is closed.

MAKING THE RULER FOLDER

1. Fold the leaf-print L rectangle in half widthwise, right sides together to make a 25" x 14¼" piece. Sew along the 25" edge, leaving the ends open. Press the seam allowances open. Turn the piece right side out. With the seam along one folded edge, press flat to make the ruler-pocket panel. Mark the center point on the open ends.

2. To make the accessory pockets, layer the leaf-print M rectangles right sides together. Sew around the edges, leaving a 2" gap on one long side. Trim the corners and turn the pocket right side out. Press the turning-gap seam allowances to the wrong side. Make a second pocket using the leaf-print N rectangles.

3. Position the M pocket on the top-left corner of one blue O rectangle, 4" down from the top edge and 2¼" in from the left side. Pin the pocket in place, making sure the turning gap is along the bottom edge. Topstitch the sides and bottom of the pocket.

4. Position the N pocket on the top-left corner of the other blue O rectangle, 4" down from the top edge and 1½" in from the left side. Pin the pocket in place, making sure the turning gap is along the bottom edge. Topstitch the sides and bottom of the pocket. Stitch a vertical line

through the pocket, 1" in from the right side to divide the pocket as shown.

5. On the right side of the tree-print P rectangle, mark the center point on both long sides. Lay the ruler-pocket panel from step 1 on top of the P rectangle, matching the marked center points. Lay one blue O rectangle right side down, aligning the top edge of the the O rectangle with one 25" side of the P rectangle. Pin in place. Lay the second blue O rectangle right side down, aligning the top edge of the O rectangle with the opposite 25" side of the P rectangle. Pin in place. *Note that the bottom edges of the O rectangles will overlap each other by ½" in the middle of the ruler folder.*

6. Sew all the way around the outside edges of the folder. Clip the corners. Turn the folder right side out through the overlapped bottom edges of the O rectangles, keeping the ruler pocket panel on the P rectangle side for now. Gently poke out the corners.

Detail of pocket N

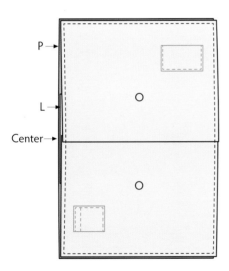

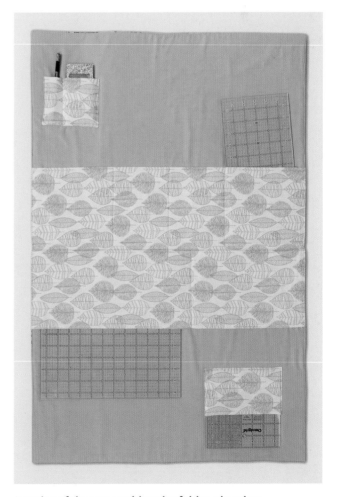

Interior of the removable ruler folder, showing pocket N, ruler-pocket panel, and pocket M.

7. Press the interfacing pieces flat and insert one through the opening between the O rectangles on each side of the ruler folder. Make sure all seam allowances sit on one side of the interfacing to avoid lumpy edges around the perimeter of the ruler folder. Glue baste the overlapped O rectangles closed. The overlap will be concealed in the next step, so there's no need to turn raw edges under.

8. When the fabric glue has dried, flip the ruler-pocket panel over to the O rectangle side. Referring to the removable ruler-folder photo on page 19, draw a straight line across the middle of the ruler-pocket panel corresponding to the fold line of the ruler folder. Sew along the line. Mark stitching lines on the pocket panel, perpendicular to the fold line, to accommodate your ruler collection. The sample shown has 14" and 10½" wide pockets for square rulers on one side of the folder and 7¼", 5", 5", and 7¼" wide pockets on the other side. A 6" x 24" ruler can lie inside the folder between the pockets.

9. If desired, topstitch around the perimeter of the folder, catching the edges of the interfacing. Stock your ruler folder; then fold it in half and insert it, fold side down, into your tote. Insert an 18" x 24" cutting mat behind the ruler folder and you're ready for retreat!

Berene Campbell

When I went on my first day-long quilting retreat, I wasn't sure what to pack. Hedging my bets, I arrived with enough fabric to sink a ship. And quickly went into a flat-out panic because I hadn't brought any batting. How was I going to finish my picnic quilt (that I hadn't started yet) by that night without batting?!

After a good hearty laugh-out-loud moment, I was reassured that "There's no way you're going to finish that quilt in one day! The most important thing is to just have fun."

And I've been doing that ever since. That picnic quilt is still sitting in my cupboard unfinished eight years later, but I had such a blast sewing with friends that I've been going on day retreats ever since.

Bigmouthed Thread Catcher

FINISHED PINCUSHION: 5" x 3½" • **FINISHED THREAD CATCHER: 8" x 7½"**

Designed and made by Krista Hennebury

Keep your sewing room or retreat-hall floor thread free with this cute thread catcher beside your machine. Nonskid slipper fabric under the pincushion and heavy filling keep this handy helper in place while you sew. Recycled fiberglass strapping holds the top of the bag wide open to catch your threads. Make one for the arm of your couch for hand-sewing projects, too! These are perfect gifts for sewing friends and are also quick sellers in quilt-show boutiques.

MATERIALS

Yardage is based on 42"-wide fabric unless otherwise noted.

1 fat quarter (18" x 21") of bright print for bag exterior and pincushion
1 fat quarter of coordinating print for bag lining, straps, and loop
2 rectangles, at least 5" x 6", of muslin for pincushion
½ yard of decorative twill tape for trim
1 piece, 5" x 6", of nonskid slipper fabric*
18" length of ¼"- or ⅜"-wide fiberglass strapping*
1 cup, or 8 ounces, of clean sand or recycled ground glass*
Fabric glue
Funnel

See "Where Do I Find That?" on page 23.

CUTTING

All measurements include a ¼" seam allowance unless otherwise noted.

From the bright print, cut:
1 rectangle, 9" x 18"
1 rectangle, 4" x 5½"

From the coordinating print, cut:
1 rectangle, 9" x 18"
1 rectangle, 3" x 6"
1 rectangle, 1" x 3"

From the muslin, cut:
2 rectangles, 4" x 5½"

From the nonskid fabric, cut:
1 rectangle, 4" x 5½"

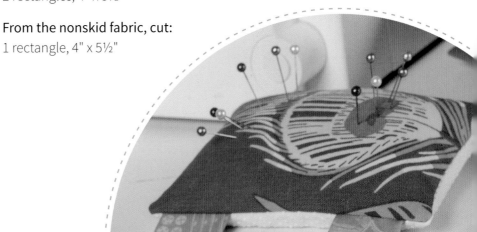

Where Do I Find That?

Fiberglass strapping is typically thrown away after it has served its purpose baling heavy boxes together. Ask for it at copy centers, florist shops, mailing depots, or from a local newspaper carrier. Ground glass is used as an industrial abrasive; find it in bulk at sandblasting companies. If it isn't available near you, clean play sand used for children's sandboxes is a great alternative and it's available at home-improvement centers. Finally, slipper fabric with tiny nonskid rubber dots is available at most large fabric-outlet stores.

MAKING THE THREAD BAG

1. Fold the bright 9" x 18" rectangle in half, right sides together, aligning the short ends as shown. Sew the ends together using a ⅜" seam allowance to make a tube. Press the seam allowances open. Center the seam, then lightly press the sides of the tube to make a crease. Sew the bottom closed to make the exterior bag.

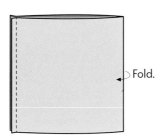
Fold.

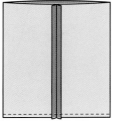
Center seam.

2. Repeat step 1 using the coordinating 9" x 18" rectangle to make the bag lining.

3. To make a gusset in the bottom corners, align the bottom seam and a side crease. Pinch the corner flat to make a triangle. Using a ruler and pencil, draw a straight line perpendicular to the seam, 1" in from the corner point. Sew along the line and then trim the corner fabric ¼" from the stitched line as shown.

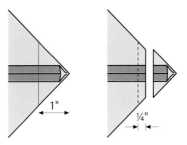

4. Turn the exterior bag right side out and gently press out the corners. With wrong sides together, insert the lining, matching the seams at the back of the bag and the raw edges around the top. Keeping the raw edges aligned, fold the raw edges down onto the exterior so that the lining makes a 1" accent hem. Press. Using a long stitch length, baste close to the raw edge all around the bag, leaving a 1" opening at the back seam.

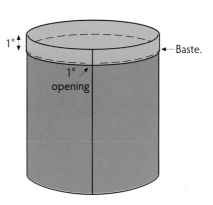

5. Using utility scissors, trim one end of the fiberglass strapping, rounding any sharp corners. Insert the strapping through the opening in the hem until it wraps all the way around the top of the bag. Overlap the strapping ends about 1" at the back of the bag, and then trim the other end of the strap, rounding any sharp corners. Insert the newly cut end inside the hem.

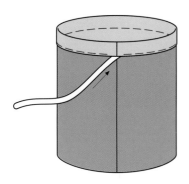

6. To make the scissor loop, fold the coordinating 1" x 3" rectangle in half lengthwise, wrong sides together, and press the fold. Unfold, turn the raw edges of the rectangle in to meet the center crease, and press the folds. Refold on the center crease again and press. Topstitch along the long side of the strip as shown.

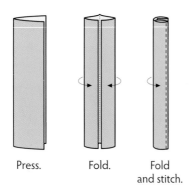

Press.   Fold.   Fold and stitch.

7. Open a few of the basting stitches along the hem on the left side of the bag. Fold the strip from step 6 in half to make a loop. With the raw ends next to each other and the same side of the loop facing up, insert about ⅜" of the raw ends under the hem. Pin or use fabric glue to secure the loop in place. Starting at the back

seam, pin the decorative twill tape around the bottom of the hem, enclosing the raw edge. Overlap the twill tape ends by ½" at the back seam. Set aside.

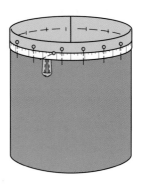

MAKING THE STRAPS AND PINCUSHION

1. Fold the coordinating 3" x 6" rectangle in half lengthwise, right sides together, to make a 1½" x 6" rectangle. Using a short stitch length and a ¼" seam allowance, sew around the three open sides, backstitching and pivoting at the corners. Cut the rectangle in half to make two 1½" x 3" tabs. Clip the corners and turn the tabs right side out, gently poking out the corners. Press.

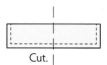

Cut. |

2. Pin the tabs in place on the right side of the nonskid fabric, ½" in from the 4" sides and with the bottom raw edges aligned as shown.

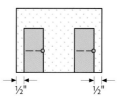

½"   ½"

3. To make the pincushion, layer the fabrics, starting at the bottom, as follows: muslin, nonskid fabric with tabs right side up, bright 4" x 5½" rectangle wrong side up, and muslin.

Pin through all the layers. Shorten the stitch length to 1.0 to 1.5 to help contain the sand filling. Beginning and ending with a backstitch, sew around the perimeter, pivoting at the corners, and leaving a 1¼" opening along the 5" side opposite the tabs. Reset your stitch length to normal.

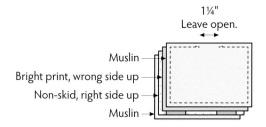

1¼"
Leave open.

Muslin
Bright print, wrong side up
Non-skid, right side up
Muslin

4. Clip corners and turn the pincushion right side out through the opening. Carefully poke out the corners and press from the top side to avoid melting the nonskid dots.

ASSEMBLING THE THREAD CATCHER

1. On the back of the exterior bag, position the pincushion tabs on either side of the seam. Align the finished edge of the tabs with the bottom edge of the twill tape, on top of the tape. Make sure the nonskid fabric is facing away from the bag. Pin the tabs in place.

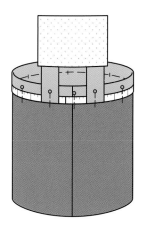

2. Remove the extension table so you can use the free arm on your sewing machine. Using thread in the top of the machine that matches the twill tape and bobbin thread that matches the lining

fabric, topstitch all around the bottom and top edges of the twill tape, sewing over the tabs at the back and securing the scissor loop. Move the fiberglass strapping out of the way inside the hem and topstitch around the top edge of the bag, again catching the tabs and securing them to the bag. Remove any basting stitches from the bag hem.

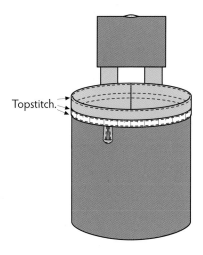

Topstitch.

3. Using a funnel, fill the pincushion with sand or crushed glass through the opening. Fill it as much as possible, shaking the pincushion to settle the filling. Close the opening with tiny ladder stitches using a double strand of thread.

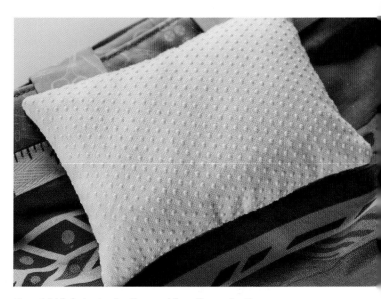

Nonskid fabric, typically used for slipper bottoms, helps to keep the thread catcher in place on your sewing table.

Double Scissor Keeper

FINISHED SIZE: 4¾" x 9½"

Designed and made by Amy Friend

Protect your shears, embroidery scissors, and the rest of your tools from damage by storing your scissors in this clever double scissor keeper. A swivel ring clasp lets you clip your keeper to the side of a larger tote or bag so that your scissors are always handy when you need them.

MATERIALS

Yardage is based on 42"-wide fabric.

½ yard of linen or home-decor fabric for exterior

1 fat quarter (18" x 21") of coordinating cotton print for lining, flap, front pocket, and swivel ring tab

2¼" x 4" rectangle of contrasting cotton print for binding

18" x 21" piece of fusible fleece

1 swivel ring clasp

1 magnetic snap

Pinking shears (optional)

CUTTING

All measurements include a ¼" seam allowance unless otherwise noted. Patterns for pieces A–C appear on pages 30 and 31.

From the linen or home-decor fabric, cut:
2 of piece A

From the coordinating cotton print, cut:
2 of piece A
2 of piece B
2 of piece C
1 rectangle, 1" x 1½"

From the fusible fleece, cut:
2 of piece A
1 of piece B
1 of piece C

PREPARING THE PATTERN PIECES

1. Fuse a fleece A piece to the wrong side of each linen or home-decor A piece. Fuse the fleece B piece to the wrong side of one coordinating B piece. Fuse the fleece C piece to the wrong side of one coordinating C piece.

2. Press the cotton 2¼" x 4" rectangle in half lengthwise, wrong sides together, to make a binding strip.

MAKING THE SCISSOR KEEPER

1. Layer the fused C piece wrong sides together with the remaining C piece. Pin the binding strip along the top edge, aligning the raw edges and making sure to pin through all of the layers. Sew the strip in place. Fold the binding to the back and hand or machine stitch in place to complete the outer pocket.

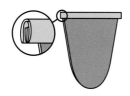

Outer pocket

2. Place the outer pocket on top of a fused A piece, right side facing up. Baste the pocket to the A piece ⅛" from the outer edge to make the exterior front piece. Trim the binding strip even with the edges of the A piece.

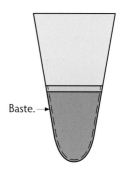

Baste. →

3. To make the swivel ring tab, fold the 1" x 1½" rectangle in half lengthwise, wrong sides together. Press the fold. Unfold, turn the raw edges of the rectangle in to meet the center crease, and press the folds. Refold on the center crease again and press. The tab should measure ¼" x 1½". Topstitch along both sides of the strip. Fold the strip in half with the raw edges aligned. Slip the swivel ring clasp through the loop. Baste the loop in place ¾" down from the top-right edge of the exterior front piece.

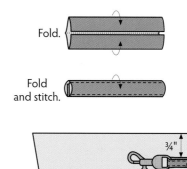

Fold.

Fold and stitch.

¾"

4. To make the flap, layer the fused B piece right sides together with the remaining B piece, aligning the raw edges. Stitch around the curve. Clip small V-notches into the curve or trim with pinking shears. Turn right side out and press. Topstitch around the finished curve. Fold the flap in half and pin-mark the center. Following the manufacturer's directions, install the male side of magnetic snap through the center of the flap lining, about ¼" from the edge of the curve.

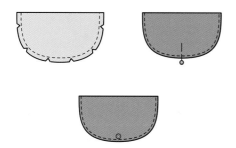

5. Center the flap on the top edge of the remaining fused A piece, right sides together and raw edges aligned. Baste ⅛" from the straight edge to make the exterior back.

Exterior back

6. With right sides together, sew the coordinating A pieces together around the curved edges, leaving the top straight edge open to make the lining. In the same way, sew the exterior front and back pieces together, using caution not to catch the flap edges or the metal hardware in the seam. Using a short stitch length, sew around the bottom curve of the exterior pieces, stitching on top of the first line of stitching to protect the seam from sharp scissor points. Carefully clip notches from the curves on both the body and the lining. Trim some of the bulk from the exterior fabric seam allowance.

7. Turn the lining right side out. Place the lining inside the exterior, right sides together and raw edges aligned. Pin along the top edge. Beginning and ending with a backstitch, sew around the top edge, leaving a 2" opening on the *front* for turning. Turn the scissor keeper right side out through the opening. Turn under the raw edges of the turning gap and press well.

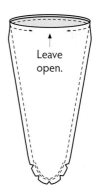

8. Insert your scissors into the scissor keeper and close the flap. Mark the spot on the exterior front that corresponds to the magnetic snap on the flap. Reach through the turning hole and install the other magnetic snap piece. Hand stitch the opening closed. Topstitch around the upper edge of the scissor keeper, making sure to avoid all of the hardware.

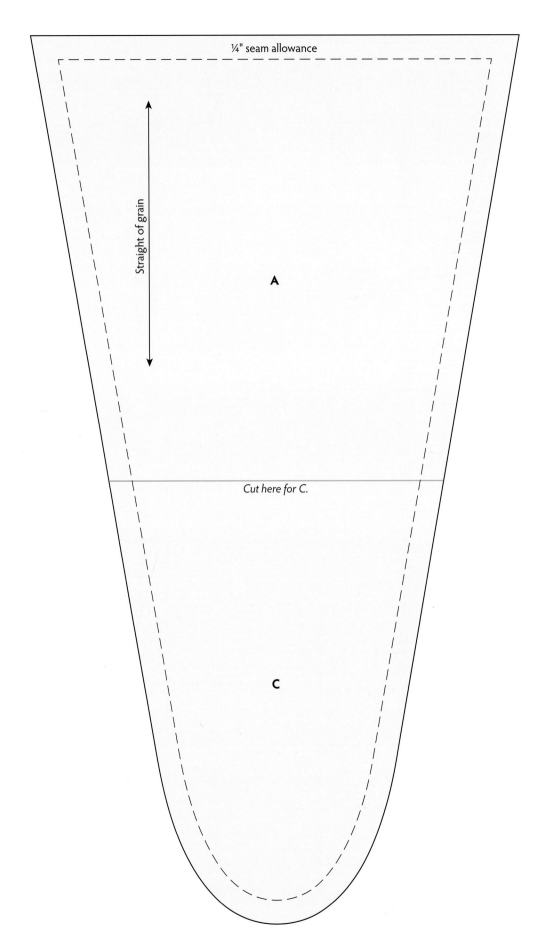

¼" seam allowance

Straight of grain

A

Cut here for C.

C

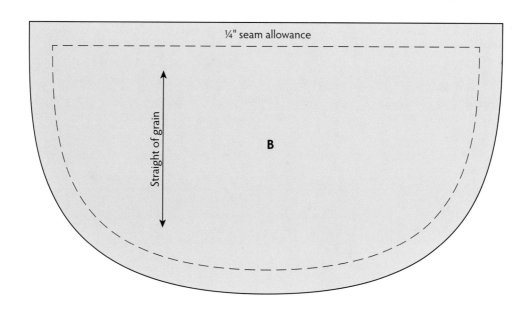

¼" seam allowance

Straight of grain

B

Amy Friend

My greatest excitement in attending my first retreat was simply getting away by myself for two nights and a full day of sewing. As it turns out, that break from parenting was very refreshing—it was wonderful to focus on sewing for big chunks of time rather than for a few minutes here and there. But what turned out to be the biggest life-changing aspect for me was the design wall.

I brought a dozen blocks made by my paper-piecing friends from all over the world to the retreat. They were different sizes, so it was challenging to set them together. It was so helpful to be able to place the blocks on the design wall, move them around, and then piece them together with irregular sashing.

When I got home, I talked nonstop about design walls until my husband figured out how to build one that I could store behind a hutch in my small sewing room.

Big and Little Patchwork Totes

FINISHED BIG TOTE: 21" wide x 13½" tall • FINISHED LITTLE TOTE: 12¾" wide x 8" tall

Designed and made by Ayumi Takahashi

Both Ayumi's signature patchwork style and her Japanese design esthetic shine through with these cute totes. The big tote is large enough to pack your favorite quilt to take along on retreat, or fill with yardage for your planned projects, while the little tote can carry your mug and snack-time necessities or be a wonderful gift bag to hold a few fat quarters for your retreat friends.

MATERIALS

Yardage is based on 42"-wide fabric unless otherwise noted.

Big Tote

¼ yard *each* of 5 assorted prints for exterior sides
¾ yard of fabric for lining
¼ yard of fabric for exterior base
⅛ yard *each* of 2 fabrics (1 print and 1 solid) for handles
½ yard of lightweight, woven fusible interfacing
1 yard of fusible fleece or heavyweight interfacing

Little Tote

1 fat eighth (9" x 21") *each* of 5 assorted prints for exterior sides
½ yard of fabric for lining
1 fat eighth of fabric for exterior base
⅛ yard *each* of 2 fabrics (1 print and 1 solid) for handles
¾ yard of lightweight, woven fusible interfacing

Additional Supplies for Both

2 sheets of copy paper
Removable fabric-marking pen or chalk

CUTTING FOR BIG TOTE

All measurements include a ¼" seam allowance unless otherwise noted. Referring to the photo above, decide the order of the assorted prints from top to bottom for the exterior sides. Label the prints 1 to 5, starting at the top.

From print #1, cut:
2 strips, 2½" x 21½"

From print #2, cut:
2 strips, 2½" x 21½"

From print #3, cut:
2 strips, 3¼" x 21½"

From print #4, cut:
2 strips, 3½" x 21½"

From print #5, cut:
2 strips, 4¼" x 21½"

From the fabric for exterior base, cut:
1 rectangle, 7" x 21½"

From the fabric for lining, cut:
2 rectangles, 17¼" x 21½"

From *each* of the fabrics for handles, cut:
2 strips, 3¼" x 16½"

From the lightweight interfacing, cut:
2 rectangles, 6" x 16½"

From the fusible fleece or heavyweight interfacing, cut:
1 rectangle, 21½" x 34"

CUTTING FOR LITTLE TOTE

A ¼" seam allowance is included in all measurements unless otherwise noted. Referring to the photo above, decide the order of the assorted prints from top to bottom for the exterior sides. Label the prints 1 to 5, starting at the top.

From print #1, cut:
2 strips, 1¾" x 13¼"

From print #2, cut:
2 strips, 2" x 13¼"

From print #3, cut:
2 strips, 2¼" x 13¼"

From print #4, cut:
2 strips, 2½" x 13¼"

From print #5, cut:
2 strips, 2½" x 13¼"

From the fabric for exterior base, cut:
1 rectangle, 4½" x 13¼"

From the fabric for lining, cut:
2 rectangles, 13¼" x 21½"

From *each* of the fabrics for handles, cut:
2 strips, 2" x 10½"

From the lightweight interfacing, cut:
2 rectangles, 13¼" x 21½"

PIECING THE TOTE BAG EXTERIOR

The process for making the big and little totes is the same, except where noted.

1. Arrange the print strips in numerical order with print #1 at the top, taking care to properly orient any directional or text prints. Sew the strips together along their long edges to make a strip set. Press the seam allowances toward the top strip. Make a second identical strip set. Press the seam allowances toward the bottom strip. The strip sets should measure 21½" x 14" for the big tote or 13¼" x 9" for the little tote.

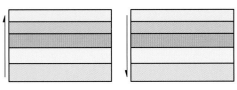

Make 1 of each.

2. Lay out the exterior base rectangle and the strip sets with the bottom strips next to the base piece. Join the pieces to make a large rectangle for the tote exterior. Press the seam allowances toward the base piece.

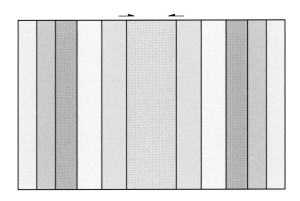

3. Following manufacturer's instructions, fuse the fleece to the wrong side of the big tote exterior *or* fuse the interfacing to the wrong side of the little tote exterior.

ASSEMBLING THE TOTE BAG

1. *For the big tote only,* join the lining pieces, right sides together, along their 21½" edges. Press the seam allowances in one direction. *For both totes,* layer the tote-bag exterior and its corresponding lining, right side together and raw edges aligned. Pin the layers together.

2. Trace the appropriate-sized pattern (pages 38 and 39) onto paper. Cut out the template, cutting along the curved lines. Position the template on one short end of the lining as shown, matching the straight edges at the side and top of the template. Trace the curves. Flip the template along the center line and continue tracing the curves. Repeat at the opposite end of the bag.

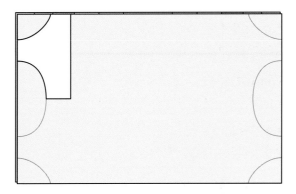

3. Pin the layers together along the marked curves. Beginning and ending with a backstitch, sew on the marked lines. Trim the excess fabric, leaving ⅜" *outside* of the curves for seam allowance to create the top edges of the tote. Clip the seam allowance along the curve, taking care to not cut into the line of stitches.

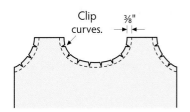

Clip curves.   ⅜"

4. Separate the lining and exterior rectangles so that the top edges of the tote meet in the center. The exterior strips should be on top of each other, with right sides together and side edges aligned as shown. Fold the exterior curved edges (at the top of the tote) over the lining so the tote is flat. Press the folds at the bottom of the exterior and the lining to make a crease.

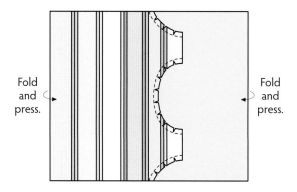

Fold and press.

Fold and press.

5. Pin the side seams, taking care to line up the exterior strips. Sew one side seam, starting at the fold of the exterior and ending at the fold of the lining. On the other side seam, backstitch and leave a 4" (big tote) *or* 3" (little tote) opening in the lining for turning.

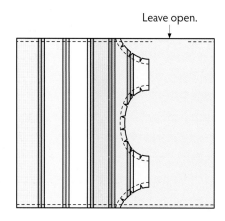

Leave open.

6. To make a gusset in the bottom corners on the exterior, place a side seam on top of the bottom crease. Pinch the corner flat to make a triangle. Using a ruler and pencil, draw a 6½" line perpendicular to the seam for the big tote *or a 4" line for the little tote. Note that on the*

exterior corners, this line corresponds to the width of the base piece. Starting and ending with a backstitch, sew along the line. Trim the corner fabric ⅜" from the stitched line. Repeat the process to make a gusset in the lining.

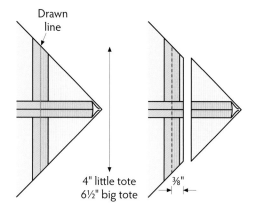

Drawn line

4" little tote
6½" big tote

⅜"

7. Gently turn the tote right side out through the opening in the lining. Press the curves along the top of the tote. Turn under all of the raw edges at the handle openings ⅜" to the wrong side and press. Turn under the raw edges of the turning gap and press. Hand stitch the opening closed.

MAKING THE HANDLES

1. Using the strips for the handles, join one solid strip and one print strip, right sides together, along one long edge as shown. Press the seam allowances open. Repeat to make a second strip set. *For the big tote only,* follow manufacturer's instructions and fuse the lightweight interfacing to the wrong side of the strip sets.

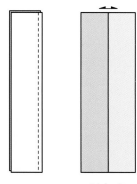

Make 2.

2. Fold the long raw edges in to the center seam, wrong sides together. Press the folds. Fold the handles in half along the seam, enclosing the raw edges, and press again. Pin and topstitch along each long side.

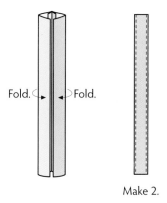

Make 2.

3. *For the big tote only,* the handles will be inserted at an angle. Make a mark ⅜" from the end of a handle on the left side. Make another mark 1" from the same end on the right side. Draw a line between the two marks. At the other end of the handle, reverse the markings as shown.

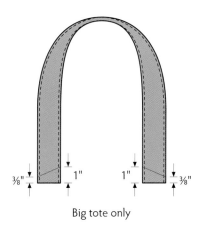

⅜" 1"   1" ⅜"

Big tote only

FINISHING THE TOTE

1. *For the big tote only,* on one side insert the handles into the openings, matching the drawn line with the pressed top edge of the handle opening. *For the little tote only,* insert the ends of one handle ⅜" into the openings on one side of the tote. Pin in place, taking care not to twist the handle or cross over the top of the tote. In the same way, pin a handle on the other side of the tote.

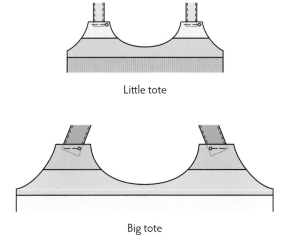

Little tote

Big tote

2. Topstitch around the entire top edge of the tote, securing the handles with a double line of stitching, if desired.

Ayumi Takahashi

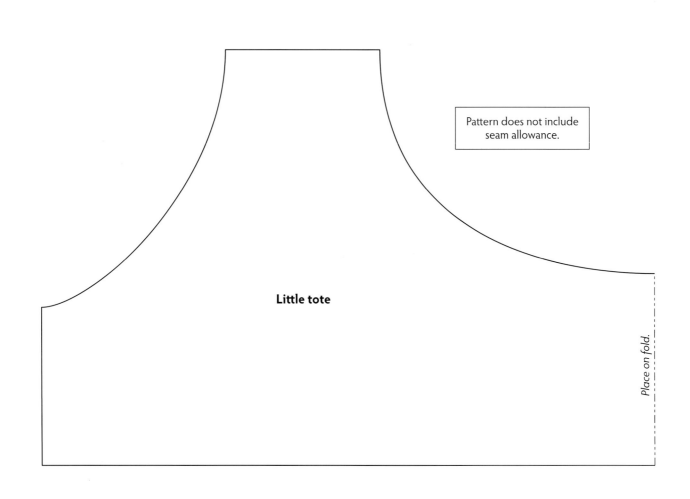

Quilting retreats aren't popular or readily available in Tokyo, where I live. I only learned about retreats from reading sewing blogs and talking to my online friends. Spending a whole weekend with friends just to enjoy sewing together sounds absolutely fantastic—a whole other level of joy!

My passion for sewing was fueled once I discovered the online sewing community. New friends to share my projects with, and to learn from, made sewing a lot more fun for me. So whether you have an actual quilting retreat in your future, or you sew on your own in your own studio, it's fun to meet new friends online to share projects and ideas.

Pattern does not include seam allowance.

Little tote

Place on fold.

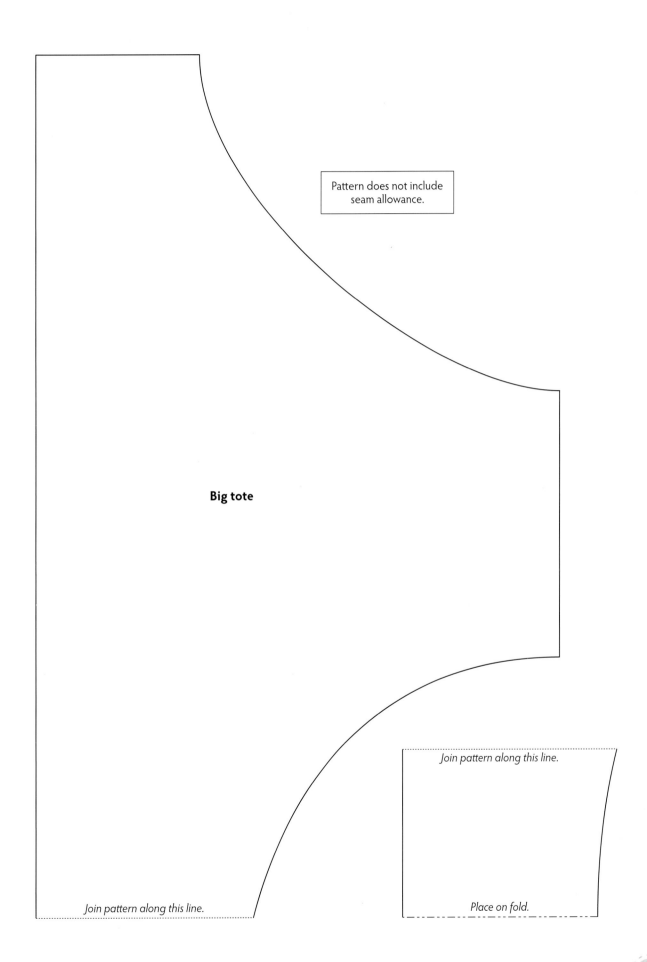

Pattern does not include seam allowance.

Big tote

Join pattern along this line.

Join pattern along this line.

Place on fold.

Join pattern along this line.

Knitwit Needle Clutch

FINISHED SIZE: 10½" x 6", closed and fastened; 15½" x 18", open

Designed and made by Kristie Maslow

Knit on the go and in style with this functional clutch designed to store and organize your knitting needles and notions. Interior pockets can be custom designed to store various sizes of interchangeable, circular, and double-pointed knitting needles. Clever vinyl pockets hold printed needle-size labels, while the pattern pocket allows a clear view of your project instructions. An outer zippered pocket is perfect for storing small notions such as stitch markers and a measuring tape.

MATERIALS

Yardage is based on 42"-wide fabric unless otherwise noted.

½ yard of linen or home-decor fabric for exterior
½ yard of gray dot for lining
⅓ yard of light-gray print for divided pockets
⅜ yard of 18"-wide mediumweight clear vinyl
10½" x 15½" piece of fusible fleece
1 yard of lightweight, woven fusible interfacing
1 nylon zipper, 7" long
1 decorative button, 1½" or larger
Sharp embroidery scissors
Removable fabric-marking pen or chalk

CUTTING

All measurements include a ½" seam allowance unless otherwise noted.

From the gray dot, cut:
1 rectangle, 11½" x 16½" (A)
1 rectangle, 9" x 16½" (B)
1 rectangle, 7½" x 16½" (C)
1 rectangle, 5" x 16½" (D)
1 rectangle, 8½" x 12" (E)

From the linen or home-decor fabric, cut:
1 rectangle, 11½" x 16½" (A)
1 rectangle, 9" x 16½" (B)
1 rectangle, 1½" x 5"

From the light-gray print, cut:
1 rectangle, 7½" x 16½" (C)
1 rectangle, 5" x 16½" (D)

Continued on page 42.

Continued from page 40.

From the interfacing, cut:
1 rectangle, 8" x 15½" (B)
1 rectangle, 6½" x 15½" (C)
1 rectangle, 4" x 15½" (D)
1 rectangle, 7½" x 11" (E)

From the vinyl, cut,
2 strips, 1" x 16½"
1 rectangle, 6½" x 9½"

Working with Vinyl

Here are some helpful tips if you have not sewn with vinyl before:

- *Secure your vinyl piece for cutting by taping at least two edges to your cutting mat with painter's tape.*

- *A Teflon foot glides smoothly over vinyl and helps maintain proper tension. If you don't have a Teflon foot, try putting a piece of cello tape on the bottom of your regular sewing foot or laying a strip of tissue paper on top of the vinyl. Sew through the tissue and simply tear it away later.*

- *Never iron directly on vinyl—it will melt! Defined creases can be eased out by blowing warm air from hair dryer over the vinyl.*

- *Pin and stitching holes made in vinyl are permanent. Measure twice, stitch once, and hold vinyl in place with paper clips, Wonder Clips by Clover, or painter's tape instead of pins.*

MAKING THE DIVIDED POCKETS

1. Center the corresponding interfacing pieces on the wrong side of the gray-dot B, C, and D rectangles (there will be ½" of fabric beyond the edges of the interfacing rectangles on all sides for seam allowance). Following the manufacturer's instructions, fuse the interfacing in place.

2. Place the light-gray C rectangle and the gray-dot C rectangle right sides together and sew along the top (long) edge to make pocket C. Press the seam allowances open. Turn right side out and press. Topstitch ⅛" from the sewn edge. In the same way, join the light-gray D rectangle and the gray-dot D rectangle to make pocket D.

3. Position a vinyl strip on top of pocket C ½" below the topstitched edge. Sew the bottom edge of the vinyl strip to the pocket, stitching approximately 1/16" from the edge of the vinyl. *Leave the top edge of the vinyl open to insert paper labels later.* In the same way, sew a vinyl strip on top of pocket D.

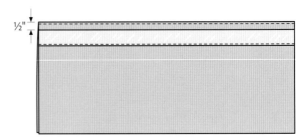

4. Following the manufacturer's instructions, center and fuse the piece of fusible fleece to the wrong side of the gray-dot A rectangle.

5. With both pieces right side up, place pocket C on top of the gray-dot A rectangle, aligning the bottom raw edges. Pin in place. Measure and mark the desired vertical sewing lines for the divided pockets using a removable fabric-marking pen (see "Suggested Pocket Widths for Knitting Needles and Supplies" on page 43).

Suggested Pocket Widths for Knitting Needles and Supplies

The sample clutch shows pockets to store an interchangeable knitting-needle set (US size 4 to 17) and has the following pocket widths.

Divided pocket C (from left to right):

- Two ¾"-wide pockets (for pencils)
- Two 2¾"-wide pockets (for 24" and 30" cables)
- Two 3"-wide pockets (for 40" and 47" cables)
- One 3½"-wide pocket

(Total width is 16½".)

Divided pocket D (from left to right):

- One 1¼"-wide pocket (for US 4 needles)
- Six ¾"-wide pockets (for US 5 to 10 needles)
- One 1"-wide pockets (for US 10.5 needles)
- Two 1¼"-wide pockets (for US 11 and 13 needles)
- Two 1½"-wide pockets (for US 15 and 17 needles)
- One 3¼"-wide pocket

(Total width is 16½".)

Other helpful pocket widths for customizing your clutch:*

- Interchangeable needles: ¾" for US sizes 4 to 9; 1" for US sizes 10 and 11; 1½" for US sizes 13 and larger
- Interchangeable cords: 2½" to 3"
- Fixed circular needles: 2½"
- Double-pointed needles: 1" for US sizes 0 to 5; 1½" for US sizes 6 to 10; 2" for US sizes 10½ to 13; and 2½" for US sizes 13 and larger
- Scissors and gauge markers: 3"–3½"
- Pens and pencils: ¾"

*For pockets along the outer raw edges, add ½" for seam allowance.

6. Stitch along the marked lines to make storage pockets in pocket C. Mark a horizontal line 5" down from the top edge of the pocket. Stitch along this line to prevent the pockets from being too deep.

7. In the same way, measure and mark the desired vertical sewing lines on pocket D as described in "Suggested Pocket Widths for Knitting Needles and Supplies" on page 43. Place pocket D on top of pocket C, aligning the bottom raw edges. Pin in place. Stitch along the marked lines to make storage pockets.

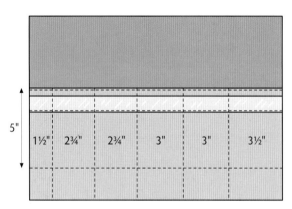

Divided pocket C

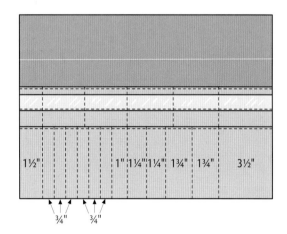

Divided pocket D

MAKING THE FLAP

1. Center the vinyl rectangle on the right side of the gray-dot B rectangle, 3½" in from each side and 1¼" from the top and bottom edges. Pin the vinyl in place, placing the pins ¼" from, and parallel to, the edge of the vinyl (this way the topstitching will cover the holes made by the pins). Sewing ¼" from the edge, stitch down one side, across the bottom, and up the other side of the vinyl pocket, removing the pins as you go.

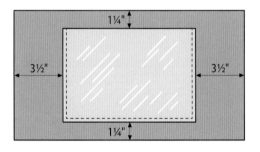

2. To make the flap, place the linen B rectangle right side together with the lining/vinyl pocket from step 1. Pin and sew along the sides and bottom edges only. Clip the corners, turn the flap right side out, and press the edges, taking care *not to press the vinyl*. Topstitch along the sides and bottom edges, leaving the top, raw edges open.

3. Align the raw edges and center the flap along the top of the piece with the divided pockets, lining sides together. Pin, and then baste along the raw edge using a scant ¼" seam allowance.

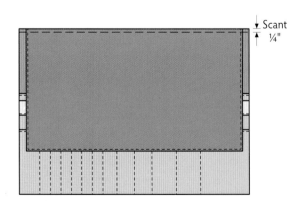

MAKING THE ZIPPER POCKET

1. Following manufacturer's directions, center and fuse the interfacing E rectangle to the wrong side of the gray-dot E rectangle. With the interfacing side facing up and an 8½" edge at the top, draw a ½" x 7" rectangle, 1½" down from the top edge and ¾" in from each side of the lining. Draw a horizontal line across the middle of the rectangle, stopping ¼" from each end.

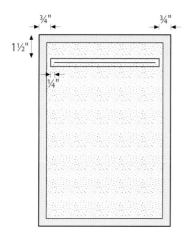

2. Position the linen or home-decor A rectangle, right side facing up with an 11½" edge at the top. With the interfacing side facing up, center the marked piece on top of the A rectangle, placing the top of the gray-dot rectangle 5" down from the top of the A rectangle as shown. Pin above and below the drawn box.

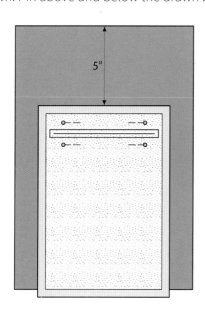

3. Using a very short stitch length, sew all the way around the marked box, pivoting with the needle down at each corner. With sharp embroidery scissors, cut along the marked center line through all layers, stopping ¼" from each end of the box. Snip diagonally into each corner, taking care not to cut into the stitched line.

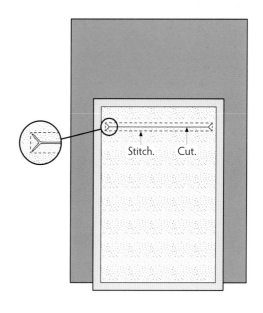

Stitch.　　Cut.

4. Push the pocket lining through the slit. Finger-press the seam, gently tugging at the corners until the lining is flat against the back of the A rectangle. Then press the box well with an iron. This creates a window for the zipper.

5. With the A rectangle right side up, place the zipper under the window with the zipper pull on the left side and the zipper end inside the box on the right side. Make sure that the zipper stops are visible in the window so that you don't sew over them and break a needle. Pin the zipper in place. Using a zipper foot, topstitch around the window as close to the finished edges as possible, sliding the zipper pull out of the way as needed.

6. On the wrong side, fold up the bottom edge of the pocket and align it with the top edge. Pin and sew around the edges of the pocket using a ¼" seam allowance, folding the exterior fabric out of the way as needed.

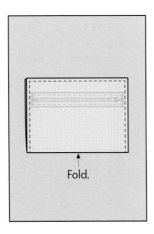

Fold.

ASSEMBLING THE CLUTCH

1. For the button loop, fold the linen 1" x 5½" rectangle in half lengthwise, wrong sides together, and press the fold. Unfold, turn the raw edges of the rectangle in to meet the center crease, refold on the center crease again, and press. Topstitch along the open side of the strip.

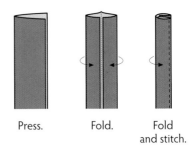

Press.   Fold.   Fold
                        and stitch.

2. Fold the strip in half with the raw ends side by side and the stitched edges facing out as shown. Center the loop on the left edge of the divided pocket panel, with the raw edges aligned. Baste the loop in place.

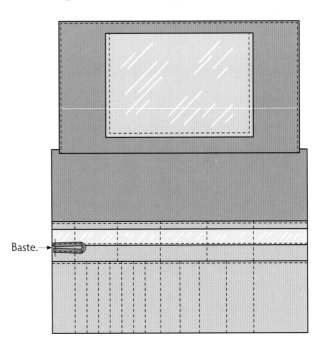

Baste.→

3. Fold the flap down over the divided pockets. Fold the corners of the flap in diagonally and pin temporarily, taking care not to pierce the vinyl, to prevent the flap corners from being sewn into the final seam.

4. Layer the exterior A rectangle right sides down on top of the flap, with the zipper pocket to the left as shown. Pin in place. Using a ½" seam allowance, sew all the way around the pieces, leaving a 4" gap on the side opposite the button loop for turning.

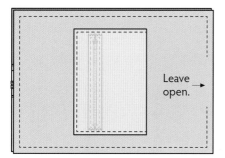

Leave open. →

5. Clip the corners and turn the clutch right side out. Gently poke out the corners. Press the edges, taking care *not to press the vinyl* and tucking in the seam allowances across the turning gap. Topstitch both short ends of the clutch, closing the turning gap.

6. With the needle pockets facing up, fold the flap down over the pockets. Fold the clutch into thirds: fold the right side toward the middle, and then the left side with the button loop overlapping the right side by about 1½".

7. Mark the center of the button loop where it overlaps the right side. Center the button on the mark and hand sew it in place through the exterior fabric only.

8. Print labels corresponding with your needle set and slide them into the vinyl pockets, then fill your clutch with needles and accessories!

Kristie Maslow

When a group of my online quilting friends decided it was time to meet in person, we flew from all over to spend a weekend in Atlanta immersed in quilting and fun.

I trotted off to the airport with my sewing machine slung over my shoulder in a handmade tote. I was heading inside when . . . SMASH! The straps on my tote gave way and my machine fell to the ground, wedged in the revolving door. I grabbed what was left of the straps and dragged the bag, sled-style, through the airport. The security guard asked what happened to my bag. I told her and she replied, "Well, you have a sewing machine; why not go find a plug and stitch it back up?" Problem was, I checked my thread with my suitcase! We dissolved into eye-watering laughter. How many people can say they laughed with airport security?

Fortunately, my machine survived, and once I arrived in Atlanta, we instantly got down to business—and fun. It was like we were all old friends, which really, we were.

Photo by Jonah O'Neil photography

Half Moon Needle Case

FINISHED SIZE (OPEN): 10½"-diameter circle

Designed and made by Leanne Chahley

This unique sewing-needle case allows you to transport full needle packets inside dedicated pockets, as well as individual needles stuck through the felt dividers. The zipper opens fully, allowing the needle book to lie flat, so you can easily find the specific needle you need. The outside features simple improvisational piecing and Leanne's signature straight-line quilting.

MATERIALS

Yardage is based on 42"-wide fabric unless otherwise noted.

Assorted scraps of prints or solids for improvisational piecing
1 fat quarter (18" x 21") of coordinating fabric for background
4 squares, 6" x 6" of wool felt for inside pockets
12" x 12" square of batting
12" x 12" square of mediumweight fusible interfacing
1 nylon zipper, 22" long
12" x 12" piece of paper for template
Compass
Removable fabric-marking pen or chalk
Fabric glue
Walking foot
Zipper foot (optional)
Clover Wonder Clips (optional)

CUTTING

All measurements include a ¼" seam allowance unless otherwise noted.

From the assorted scraps, cut:
10 to 12 strips, ¾" to 2½" wide x 6" long

From the background fabric, cut:
1 square, 11½" x 11½"
10 to 12 strips, 1" to 3½" wide x 6" long
1 rectangle, 2" x 3"

From the interfacing, cut:
1 circle, 11" diameter

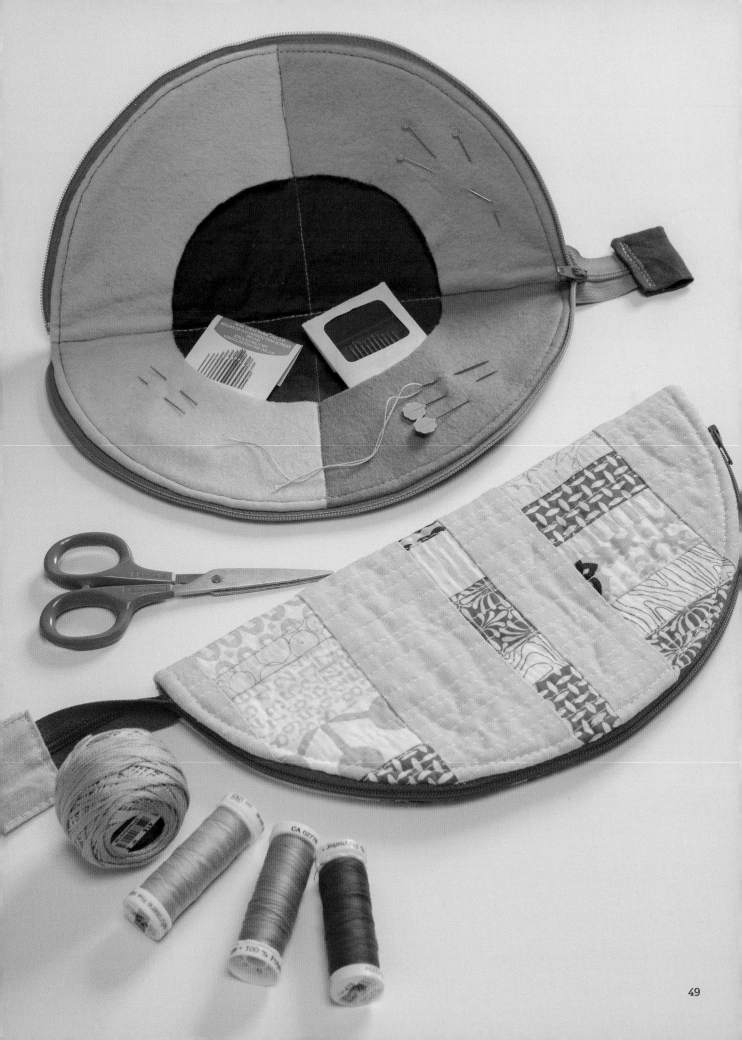

Handle With Care

Wool felt will stretch if manipulated, so work carefully and don't pull on it as you turn the project right side out. Use a pressing cloth over the felt and batting and press with care to avoid scorching the fibers.

MAKING THE OUTER CIRCLE

1. Randomly sew the assorted strips together to make a strip set that measures about 6" x 6". Press the seam allowances in one direction (or press them open if you prefer). Make two. Crosscut the strip sets into seven segments varying in width from ¾" to 3". (In the sample on page 51, the cut widths were ¾", 1", 1¼", 1½", 2", 2½", and 3".)

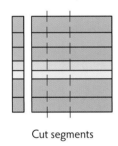

Cut segments

2. Lay out the background 6"-long strips and the segments from step 1, alternating them as shown. Join the strips and segments to make a block that measures at least 11½" wide. Press the seam allowances toward the background strips. Repeat to make a second block.

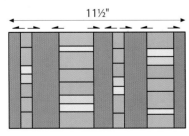

11½"

Make 2.

3. Trim the edges of the blocks (perpendicular to the long seams). Sew the blocks together along the trimmed edges. Press the seam allowances open.

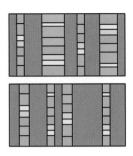

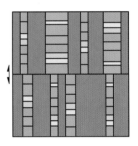

4. Place the piece from step 3 right side up on the batting square. Using a walking foot and longer stitch length, quilt as desired. The sample is quilted with straight lines ¼" apart and parallel to the center seam.

5. Use a compass to draw an 11"-diameter circle on the paper. Cut out the circle on the drawn line to make a template. Fold the circle template in half and crease the fold.

6. Place the circle template on the quilted block, matching the template fold with the center seam. Pin in place. Using a fabric-marking pen, trace around the circle directly onto the quilted piece. Remove the paper template.

7. Using a walking foot, stitch around the edge of the circle approximately ⅛" *inside* the marked line. Then cut out the circle on the marked line using fabric scissors.

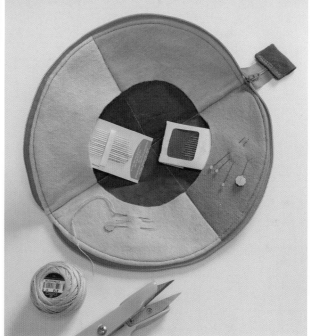

MAKING THE LINING AND FELT POCKETS

1. Following the manufacturer's instructions, center and fuse the interfacing circle onto the wrong side of the background square. Trim the excess fabric from around the interfacing circle. Fold the circle in half, wrong sides together, and press. Unfold the circle and fold the circle perpendicular to the first fold; press again to create two perpendicular creases.

2. Fold the circle template in half to make a half-circle. Fold the half-circle in half again to make a quarter-circle. Using a compass, draw an arc 2¼" from the center of the circle as shown. Cut along the drawn arc. Unfold the paper to make a donut-shaped template with four creases.

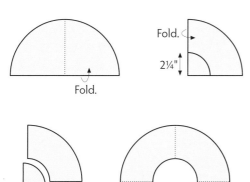

Fold.

Fold.

2¼"

Cut on marked line.

3. Cut along two adjacent creases of the donut-shaped template to make a quarter-circle arc. Use this template to cut one arc from each wool square, making sure to add a ¼" seam allowance beyond each straight edge of the template as shown. Make a total of four wool arcs.

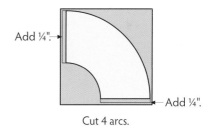

Add ¼".

Add ¼".

Cut 4 arcs.

4. Sew the wool arcs together along their straight edges to make a circle. Press the seam allowances open (see "Handle With Care" on page 50).

5. With right sides facing up, center the wool circle atop the background circle from step 1, aligning the wool seams with the creased lines on the background circle. Stitch along the wool seams and across the circle, horizontally

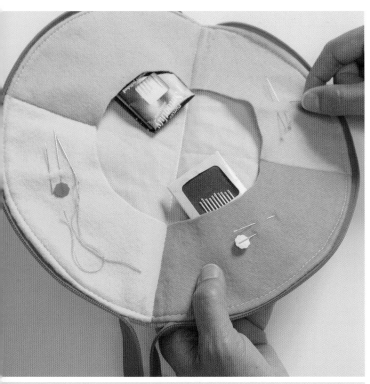

and vertically as shown. Flip the piece over and trim away any wool that extends beyond the background circle.

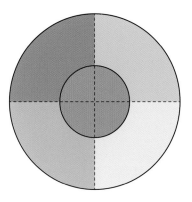

ASSEMBLING THE NEEDLE CASE

1. Using a fabric-marking pen, mark dots on the outside edge of the wool circle, ½" from each side of one seam line. Repeat at the opposite end of the same seam line. These will be the points where the zipper opens and closes.

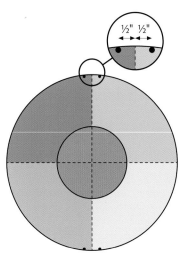

Mark dots ½" from seam.

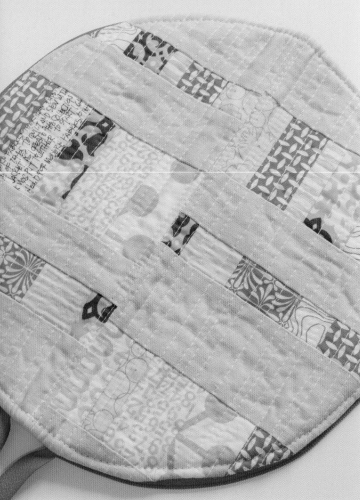

2. Open the zipper fully. Place the two zipper stops on the marks at one end of the seam line and the zipper pull on the marks at the opposite end of the seam line. Pin both ends of the zipper in place. With the zipper teeth pointing toward the middle of the circle, ease one side of the zipper tape around the outside edge of the wool circle. Pin in place. Repeat with the other side of zipper tape. Angle the ends of the zipper off the circle at the marks.

3. Using a walking foot or zipper foot, baste the zipper to the wool circle using a ⅛" seam allowance. Begin sewing at one of the zipper stop marks. Sew around one side of the circle and stop sewing when you reach the mark at the other end of the zipper, easing the tape around the edge of the circle as you sew. Remove the pins. Baste the other side of the zipper to the other side of the wool circle.

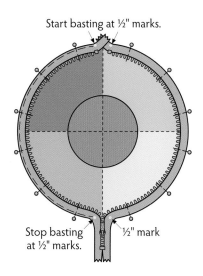

Start basting at ½" marks.

Stop basting at ½" marks.   ½" mark

4. Press the quilted circle in half along the center seam. Open the circle and fold it in half in the other direction and pin-mark the fold.

5. Place the quilted circle atop the wool circle, right sides together and aligning the seam on the quilted circle with the seam at the top and bottom of the zipper. Place the zipper's bottom end and pull between the two circles

so that you don't sew over the zipper. The top ends of the zipper tape should remain outside the circles. Pin the circles together (or use Wonder Clips), matching the wool seams with side pins on the quilted circle. Using a walking foot and a ¼" seam allowance, sew the circles together, leaving a 3" opening for turning along one side, away from either end of the zipper.

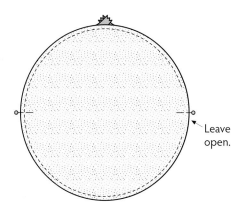

Leave open.

6. Turn the project right side out through the opening. Remember not to pull on the wool. Gently tug on the zipper teeth all around the circle to pull out the seams nicely. Press from the quilted side, tucking in the seam allowances along the opening. Hand stitch the opening closed, taking care to catch the wool, zipper tape, and quilted outer circle as you sew. Press again.

FINISHING THE NEEDLE CASE

1. With the quilted circle facing up, use a walking foot to topstitch around the circle, about ⅛" from the edge.

2. With the wool pockets facing up, stitch along the seam line that runs from the top to the bottom of the zipper, backstitching at each end. This will anchor the exterior and lining of the needle case together. Fold the needle case along the center seam and close the zipper to test it.

3. To make a zipper tab, fold under ¼" on all four sides of the background rectangle and press. Fold the rectangle in half, wrong sides together and short ends aligned. Press the fold.

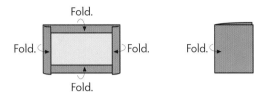

4. Open the zipper fully and lay the needle case flat. Measure 2½" down the zipper from the edge of the circle. Move the zipper pull inside the 2½" mark. Cut the zipper at the mark.

5. Insert the cut end of the zipper fully into the fabric tab. Pin in place or secure with fabric glue. Sew all the way around the fabric tab to close to the folded edges and enclose the end of the zipper.

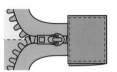

Leanne Chahley

My first quilting retreat was an adventure—and rather far from home. I packed up my sewing kit and flew halfway across the globe, from western Canada to London, England. I was a bit nervous about traveling so far to hang out with people I only knew online. But I'm so glad I went!

Every person I met was friendly, inclusive, and great fun. We talked about quilting, fabrics, blogging, and the Internet quilting community. Our common quilting interest allowed us to become friends quickly, and soon we were also sharing our histories, dreams, and challenges. We shared our knowledge and creativity, both in class and during free sewing, meals, and late-night gatherings. I found myself laughing all the time! The friendships I made at the retreat continue today, despite the distance between our homes.

Whether you go thousands of miles or just down the street, I highly recommend attending a quilting retreat. It's so much fun to set aside life's commitments and focus, just for a day or a weekend, on the love of quilting with other quilters.

Crafter's Retreat Apron

FINISHED SIZE: 9" x 19½", with ties approximately 41" long

Designed and made by Krista Fleckenstein

Quilters on retreat tend to take full advantage by spreading out and working on more than one project at a time. Things can get a little chaotic after a couple of days and tools are known to wander or become buried under stacks of fabric. Keep your tools close at hand with this multi-pocketed apron as you move from sewing machine, to cutting table, to ironing station. There's a handy loop for your glasses, a swivel hook for your snips, and even a candy pocket!

MATERIALS

Yardage is based on 42"-wide fabric unless otherwise noted.

½ yard of green dot for pocket and waist ties
1 fat quarter (18" x 21") of dark-gray print for apron front
1 fat quarter of gray stripe for waistband
¼ yard of muslin for pocket panel backing
4 squares, 6" x 6", of assorted prints for pockets
⅜ yard of canvas for apron back
1 rectangle, at least 6" x 7", of light-gray print for pocket and tabs
¾ yard of 20"-wide lightweight, woven fusible interfacing
Swivel hook with ½" opening

CUTTING

All measurements include a ¼" seam allowance unless otherwise noted.

From the assorted prints, cut:
2 rectangles, 3" x 6" (A and G)
1 rectangle, 5" x 6" (B)
1 rectangle, 2½" x 6" (C)
1 rectangle, 3½" x 6" (D)

From the light-gray print, cut:
1 rectangle, 2" x 6" (E)
1 rectangle, 2" x 4½"
1 rectangle, 1½" x 7"

From the green dot, cut:
2 strips, 3½" x 42"
1 square, 6" x 6" (F)

From the muslin, cut:
1 rectangle, 6" x 22"

Continued on page 57.

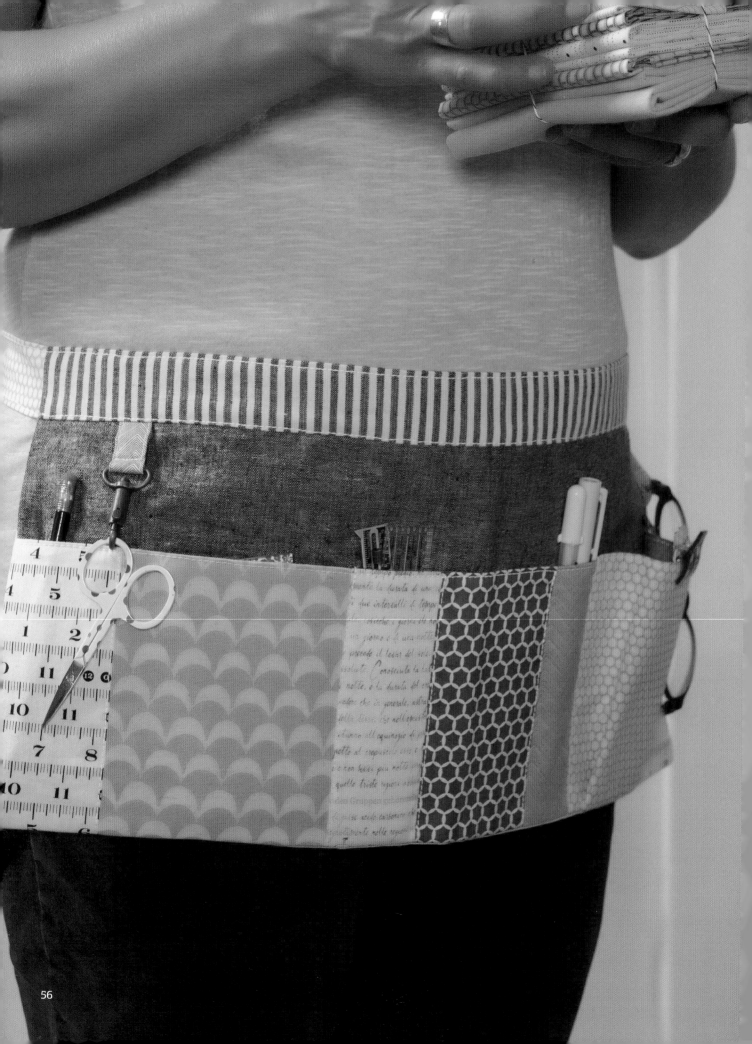

Continued from page 55.

From the interfacing, cut:

1 piece, 6" x 22"

From the dark-gray print, cut:

1 rectangle, 9½" x 20"

From the canvas, cut:

1 rectangle, 9½" x 20"

From the gray stripe, cut:

1 rectangle, 3½" x 20"

MAKING THE POCKET PANEL

1. Sew the A–G rectangles together to make the pocket panel. The pocket panel should measure 6" x 22". Press the seam allowances in one direction.

2. Following the manufacturer's directions, fuse the interfacing to the wrong side of the muslin rectangle. With right sides together, sew the pocket panel and muslin rectangle together along the top edge only. Press the seam allowances open. Turn the pieces wrong sides together and press the seam. Topstitch ⅛" from the seam along the top edge.

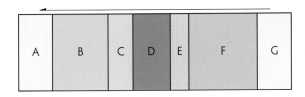

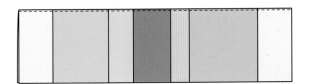

3. Pin the raw edges of the pocket panel together. Using a longer stitch length, baste along both sides and bottom edges about ⅛" from the outer edge.

4. To create the pleated pocket on the F rectangle, along the bottom of the rectangle measure ½" in from the side and make a mark. Measure 1" from the first mark and make a second mark. Fold the second mark toward the first mark and pin in place. Repeat to mark and fold the opposite side of the pocket. Sew across the bottom edge of the pocket to secure the folds, making sure to keep the raw edges aligned.

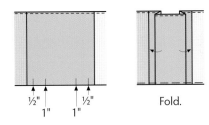

MAKING THE APRON BODY

1. Place the pocket panel right side up on top of the dark-gray rectangle, aligning the bottom edges. Pin in place. Topstitch along each pocket seam beginning at the top with a backstitch.

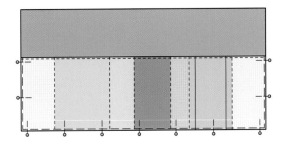

2. With right sides together, pin and sew the piece from step 1 to the canvas rectangle along the side and bottom edges to make the apron body. Trim the bottom corners. Turn the apron right side out and press.

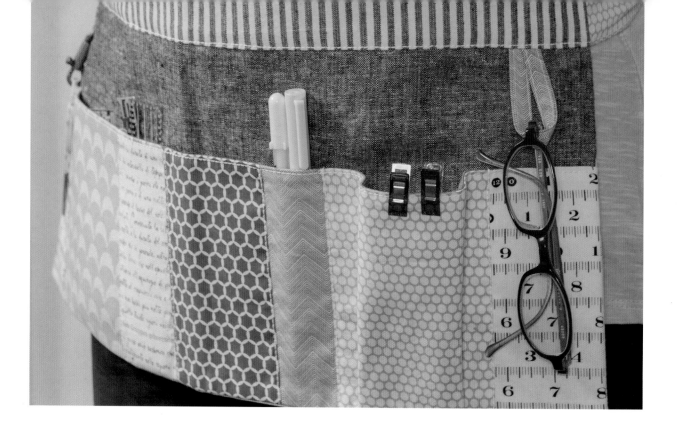

3. To make the tab for hanging glasses, fold the light-gray 1½" x 7" rectangle in half lengthwise, wrong sides together, and press the fold. Unfold, turn the raw edges of the rectangle in to meet the center crease, and press the folds. Refold on the center crease again and press. Topstitch along both sides of the strip. The tab should measure ⅜" x 7".

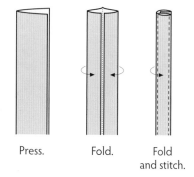

Press.   Fold.   Fold and stitch.

4. Fold the tab in half with the raw ends side by side as shown in the apron body assembly diagram at right. Aligning the raw edges, pin the tab in place at the top of the apron front,

2" in from the left or right side of the apron depending on your preference. Baste the tab in place.

5. To make the swivel hook tab, repeat step 3 using the light-gray 2" x 4½" rectangle. Slip the tab through the metal hook and align the raw edges of the tab. Stitch and backstitch across the tab as close to the metal hook as possible to secure it. Pin the tab in place at the top of the main apron front, 3" in from the opposite side of the glasses tab. Baste the tab in place.

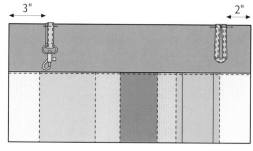

Apron body assembly

MAKING THE WAISTBAND AND TIES

1. Sew a green-dot strip to each short end of the gray striped rectangle to make a long pieced strip. Press the seam allowances toward the green strips.

2. Fold the pieced strip from step 1 in half lengthwise, right sides together with the raw edges aligned. Starting at one seam with a backstitch, sew along the bottom and side edges of one green strip and backstitch at the end of the seam. Repeat on the other green strip. The edge of the gray-striped rectangle remains open to make the apron waistband.

Leave open.

3. Clip the corners at the end of the ties. Turn your pieced strip right side out. Gently poke out the tie corners and press, folding the open edges of the gray-striped rectangle under ¼".

FINISHING THE APRON

1. Insert the apron body into the opening of the waistband all the way to the top fold of the waistband. Pin the apron and waistband securely together.

2. Topstitch all the way around the waistband and the ties, securing the waistband to the apron. Take care to catch the bottom folded edge of the waistband on the front and back of the apron.

Krista Fleckenstein

In 2011 I went on my first retreat at Loon Lake, British Columbia, Canada. It was such an eye-opening experience! I got to meet so many incredible women whom I had only known through the online quilting community, and we became even better friends than before. The energy was incredible with 28 women all creating things in the same room. Living in Alaska can be a bit isolating. Being a stay-at-home mom to four children can be, too. At retreat I was able to roll out of bed and sew in my pajamas, to stay awake into the wee hours laughing with friends, and to have those few days to feed my creative soul. It was so recharging. I'm determined to make this retreat and others an annual commitment to myself.

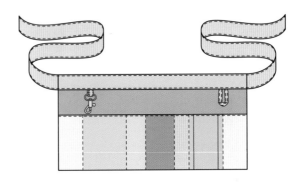

Selvage Sewing Mat

FINISHED SIZE: 18" x 18"

Designed and made by Cindy Wiens

Designed to sit under your sewing machine, this mat can help reduce "machine bounce" that often happens when sewing on long banquet tables at retreat. The mat also makes it easy to slide your machine aside when you need space on your table. The clear vinyl pockets are designed to keep your most-used tools visible, organized, and close at hand. Selvage edges, the part of the fabric usually discarded before starting a quilting project, actually can be quite artful. Recognizing the growing popularity of selvage projects, some fabric designers are even including cute little symbols on the selvages. Save your selvages for this quick retreat project!

MATERIALS

Yardage is based on 42"-wide fabric unless otherwise noted.

⅔ yard of muslin for foundation
16 to 20 assorted selvage strips, at least 1½" x 20", for mat*
1 fabric scrap, at least 1" x 20", for mat
¼ yard of multicolored print for binding
⅔ yard of fabric for backing
20" x 20" piece of batting
5" x 18" piece of mediumweight vinyl
Clover Wonder Clips or plastic-coated jumbo paper clips
Hera marker (optional)

Piece shorter strips end to end, as needed, to make 20"-long strips.

CUTTING

All measurements include a ¼" seam allowance unless otherwise noted.

From the muslin, cut:
1 square, 20" x 20"

From the backing fabric, cut:
1 square, 20" x 20"

From the multicolored print, cut:
1 strip, 1" x 18"
3 strips, 2¼" x 42"

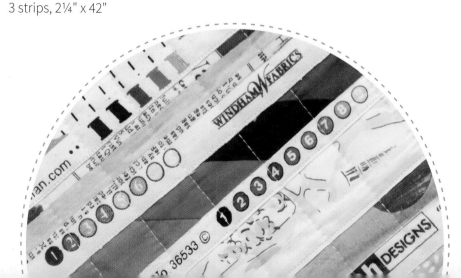

PREPARING THE FOUNDATION

With a light pencil or fabric marker, draw horizontal lines, 1½" apart, across the muslin square. Use these lines as a guide for placing the selvage strips.

Save Your Selvage

Selvages are most useful in sewing projects if at least ½" to 1" of printed fabric remains above the selvage information. I wait to trim the selvage from yardage or fat quarters until I'm going to use the yardage in a project. When trimming selvage from yardage, line up the 1½" line of your ruler with the finished selvage edge and cut. Sort your selvage stash by color, designer, fabric line, or even the printed words. Check out Cindy's blog for other creative project ideas for your selvage collection: liveacolorfullife.net.

MAKING THE MAT

1. Begin by placing the scrap 1" x 20" strip on top of the muslin foundation, right side up. The strip should be parallel to the drawn lines and aligned with the bottom edge of the foundation.

2. Place the first selvage strip on the foundation; the finished edge of the selvage strip should overlap the scrap strip ½". Pin in place. Topstitch along the finished edge of the selvage strip, securing it to the foundation.

3. Position the next selvage strip on the foundation; the finished edge of the second selvage strip should overlap the first strip ⅛" to ¼". Pin in place. Topstitch along the finished edge of the second strip. Continue adding selvage strips in the same way until the entire foundation is covered.

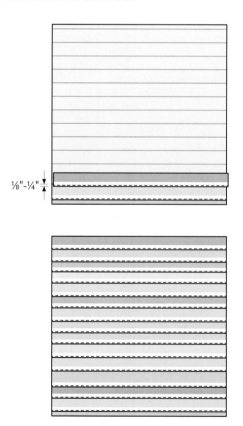

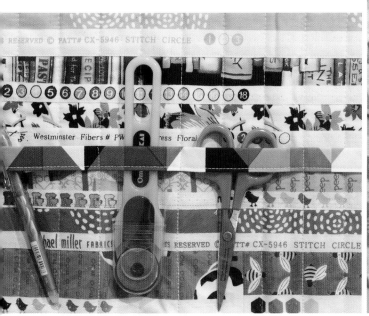

4. Layer the finished piece from step 3 with batting and backing. Baste the layers together using your preferred method

5. Quilt the mat as desired. The sample mat was quilted with parallel vertical lines about 1" apart. You may want to lengthen the stitch to 3.5 or 4 on your machine.

6. Trim the edges of the mat to measure 18" x 18".

MAKING THE VINYL GADGET POCKETS

See "Working With Vinyl" (page 42).

1. To make the binding for the top of the vinyl pocket, fold the multicolored 1" x 18" strip in half lengthwise, wrong sides together, and press the fold. Unfold, turn the raw edges of the strip in to meet the center crease, and press the folds. Refold on the center crease again and press.

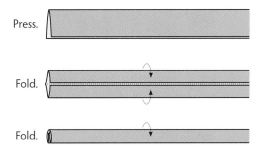

2. Insert the long edge of the vinyl into the binding, up to the center fold. Use clips to hold the binding in place and to keep it from shifting. Topstitch along the open side of the binding strip.

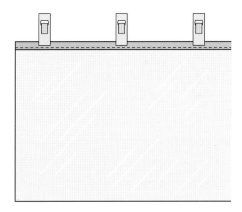

3. Place the vinyl on the selvage mat, aligning the bottom edges. Use clips on each side and along the bottom to keep it from shifting.

4. To make the gadget pockets, mark sewing lines by making a groove in the vinyl with the back of a butter knife or Hera marker. On the sample mat, lines were marked 3", 5", and 8" in from the left edge, but you can customize the width of pockets depending on your tools. You may want narrow pockets for pens or turning tools. Sew on the marked lines, stitching through the vinyl and mat.

FINISHING THE MAT

For more information on binding, go to ShopMartingale.com/HowtoQuilt for free illustrated instructions. Use the multicolored 2¼"-wide strips to bind the edges of the mat as you would a quilt.

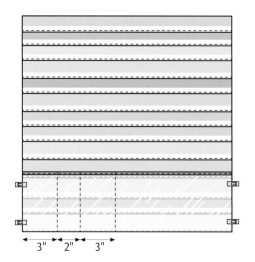

3"   2"   3"

Cindy Wiens

I have attended quilting retreats both large and small, but the most memorable is the one that I spent with my friend Dotty at her cabin just outside Yosemite National Park. We arrived late Friday night, only to have to haul all our food and sewing gear through knee-deep snow to the front door. We spent Saturday sewing, chatting, eating, and looking forward to more sewing on Sunday before we left late in the afternoon. Our sewing projects were left out when we went to bed Saturday night, ready to tackle in the morning.

Surprise! We were awakened early Sunday morning by Dotty pounding on our bedroom doors, telling us we had to pack and leave in 30 minutes. It had snowed all night and if we didn't get out of there ASAP we would be snowed in. (That actually sounded pretty good to me.) In those 30 minutes, we dressed, packed all our sewing gear, cleaned out the fridge, and then threw everything into the car, again tromping through deep snow. Dotty had the car going even before the last car door was shut. Now, 14 years later, we plan our annual retreat during warmer months!

Posy Pillow

FINISHED PILLOW COVER: 17½" x 17½" • FINISHED BLOCK: 8" x 8"

Designed and made by Amy Friend

"Posy Pillow" is an approachable project for someone new to the technique of paper foundation piecing because no points need to match. Quilters experienced in this technique can also have fun with the pattern; it provides great opportunities for fussy cutting. When choosing your fabrics, pay attention to the intensity of the color and place bolder or darker shades (print #1) along the prominent X shape and in the center diamond (print #2).

MATERIALS

Yardage is based on 42"-wide fabric unless otherwise noted.

⅓ yard of white solid for block background and border
1 fat quarter (18" x 21") of medium-pink print for blocks
1 fat eighth (9" x 21") of dark-pink print #1 for blocks
1 fat eighth of light-pink solid for blocks
1 fat eighth of medium-pink solid for blocks
1 rectangle, 3" x 6", of dark-pink print #2 for blocks
1 fat quarter of floral print for pillow back
½ yard of fusible fleece, such as HeatnBond Fleece Fusible
1 invisible zipper, 16" long
18" x 18" pillow form
Zipper foot
Size 90/14 sewing-machine needle

Sizing Pillow Covers

Many commercial pillow forms are very full in the middle, but spare around the edges. For a nice plump pillow, size your covers ½" smaller than the pillow form you plan to use. To keep the corners from collapsing, stuff a handful of fiberfill into each corner of your pillow cover before inserting the pillow form.

CUTTING

All measurements include a ¼" seam allowance unless otherwise noted.

From the white solid, cut:
2 strips, 1¼" x 42"; crosscut into:
    2 strips, 1¼" x 16½"
    2 strips, 1¼" x 18"

From the dark-pink print #2, cut:
2 squares, 3" x 3"; cut the squares in half diagonally
    to yield 4 triangles (F)

From the fusible fleece, cut:
1 square, 20" x 20"

From the floral print, cut:
1 square, 18" x 18"

MAKING THE BLOCKS

The flower is made of four identical blocks. For more information on paper-foundation-piecing techniques, go to ShopMartingale.com/HowtoQuilt for free illustrated instructions.

1. Photocopy or trace four copies of each foundation pattern on pages 70 and 71 onto lightweight paper.

2. Adding a ½" seam allowance on all sides, cut fabric pieces large enough to cover the corresponding area on the foundation paper, as follows:

    Piece A1: dark-pink print #1

    Pieces B1 and E1: medium-pink print

    Piece C1: light-pink solid

    Piece D1: medium-pink solid

    Pieces A2, A3, A4, B2, C2, D2, and E2: white solid

3. Using a size 90/14 needle and a reduced stitch length, paper piece each unit in numerical order in the colors indicated on the pattern. Press and trim after adding each piece, making sure to leave a ¼" seam allowance. Trim away any excess fabric and paper extending beyond the outer dashed line of each unit. Make four of each unit.

4. Referring to the block layout diagram, sew unit A to unit B, and then add unit C. Sew unit E to unit A, and then add unit D. Sew a dark-pink #2 F triangle to the corner of the block as shown. After sewing each seam, press the seam allowances toward the newly added unit. Trim the block to measure 8½" x 8½". Make a total of four blocks.

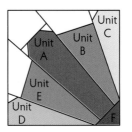

Block layout
Make 4.

5. Join the blocks as shown in the pillow-cover layout diagram to complete the flower. Press the seam allowances open. Remove the paper foundations.

6. Sew white 1¼" x 16½" strips to opposite sides of the flower. Press the seam allowances toward the border. Sew 1¼" x 18" strips to the top and bottom of the flower. Press the seam allowances toward the border.

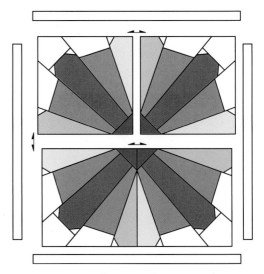

Pillow-cover layout

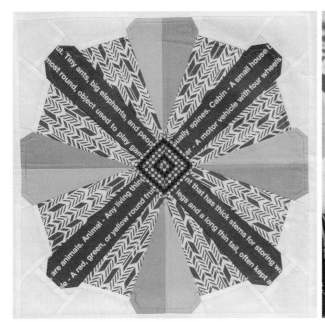

Invisible zipper inserted at pillow edge.

FINISHING THE PILLOW COVER

1. Following the manufacturer's instructions, fuse the pillow front to the fusible fleece square. Quilt as desired.

Why Use Fusible Fleece?

Fusing your pillow top to polyester fleece instantly prepares it for quilting by basting and securing the seams in one step. In addition, the fleece won't shrink. If your cotton fabric was prewashed, your pillow cover will retain its size after washing and still fit your pillow form! No backing fabric is necessary inside a pillow cover. Minimal quilting is required to stabilize the piecing. Amy simply quilted through the pillow top and batting by stitching in the ditch around the center diamond, and then echo quilted ¼" outside the center diamond and ¼" inside the flower shape.

2. Using a zipper foot, sew the invisible zipper to the bottom edges of the pillow front and back. Open the zipper halfway. With right sides together, sew the pillow front to the back along the three remaining sides, overlapping the ends of the zipper seams by ¼" at the bottom corners.

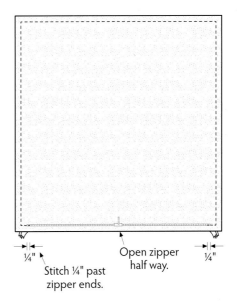

¼"

Stitch ¼" past zipper ends.

Open zipper half way.

¼"

3. Zigzag stitch over the raw edges outside the stitched line so the edges won't fray. Clip the corners and turn the pillow cover right side out; press. Insert the pillow form through the opening.

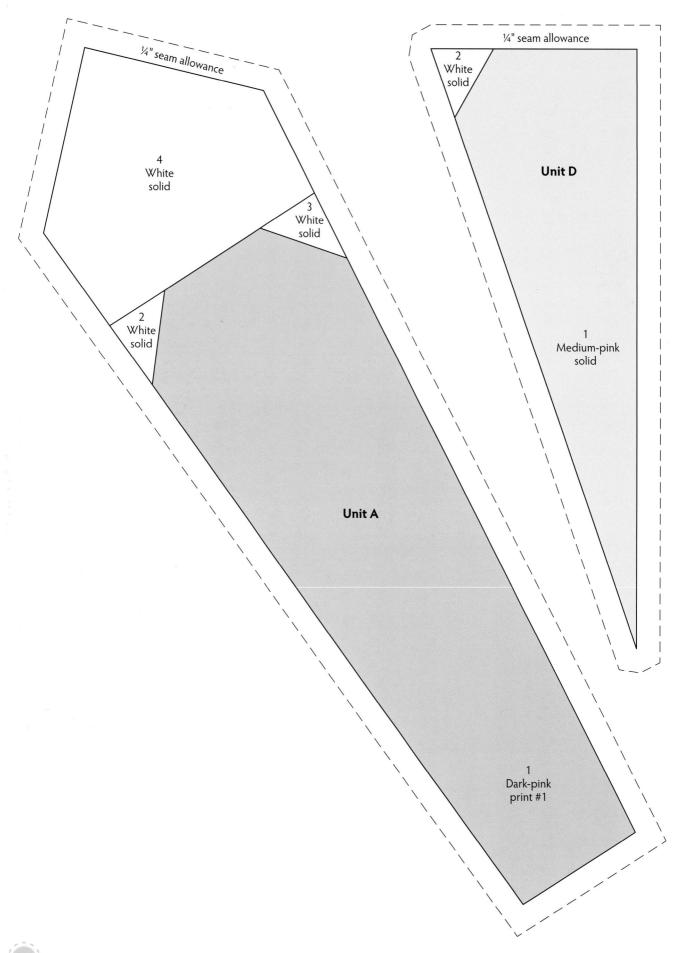

¼" seam allowance

4
White
solid

3
White
solid

2
White
solid

Unit A

1
Dark-pink
print #1

¼" seam allowance

2
White
solid

Unit D

1
Medium-pink
solid

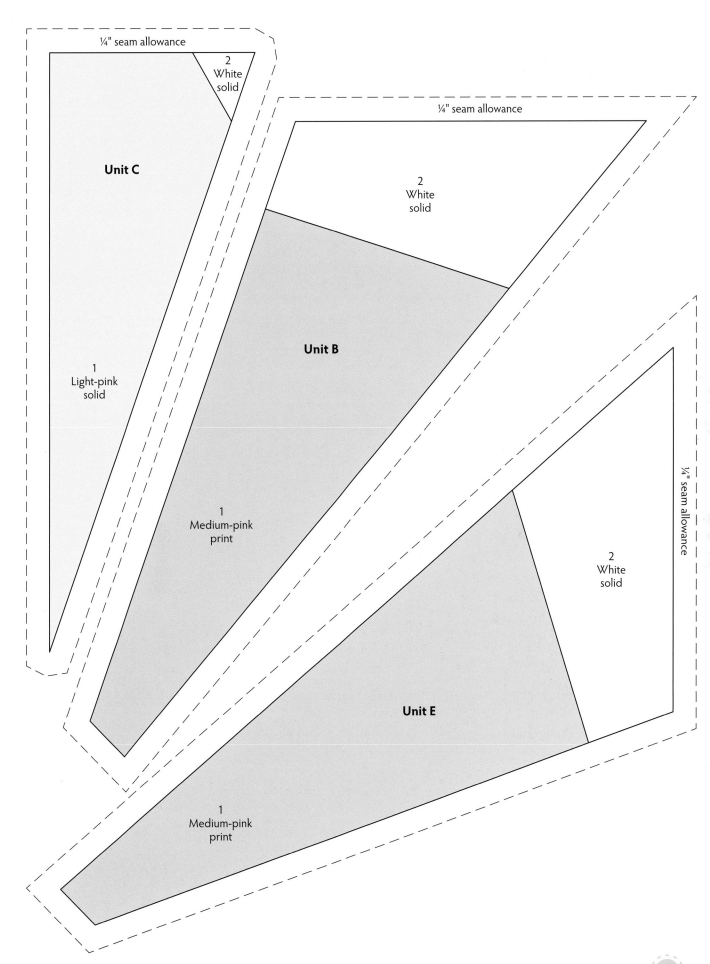

¼" seam allowance

2
White
solid

Unit C

1
Light-pink
solid

¼" seam allowance

2
White
solid

Unit B

1
Medium-pink
print

¼" seam allowance

2
White
solid

Unit E

1
Medium-pink
print

Stepping Stones Table Runner

FINISHED TABLE RUNNER: 15½" x 45½" • FINISHED BLOCK: 15" x 15"

Designed by Krista Hennebury and Krista Withers, made by Krista Hennebury, and quilted by Krista Withers

Piece and *quilt this charm-pack friendly table runner at your next day retreat or sew-in. This may be a small project, but it packs a graphic punch! Basic geometric shapes pieced into a linen background are arranged to mimic a sweet garden path along the length of the runner. Experienced quilters will appreciate the simplicity of construction and minimal time commitment to achieve beautiful results. Beginners can practice their piecing accuracy, try a new machine-appliqué technique, and then give "Quilting with Ghost Shapes" (page 78) a try!*

MATERIALS

Yardage is based on 42"-wide fabric unless otherwise noted.

¾ yard of linen or beige solid for background
20 squares, 5" x 5", of assorted prints for flying-geese units, circles, and squares
⅓ yard of multicolored print for binding
1½ yards of fabric for backing
18" x 48" piece of batting
¼ yard of 20"-wide lightweight, woven fusible interfacing
Removable fabric-marking pen
Pinking shears

CUTTING

All measurements include a ¼" seam allowance unless otherwise noted.

From the assorted prints, cut:
7 rectangles, 2½" x 4½"
6 squares, 3" x 3"
2 of circle A
2 of circle B
3 of circle C

From the linen or beige solid, cut:
1 strip, 2½" x 42"; crosscut into 14 squares, 2½" x 2½"
1 strip, 3" x 42"; crosscut into 6 squares, 3" x 3"
1 strip, 16" x 42"; crosscut into:
    1 square, 16" x 16"
    2 rectangles, 2" x 15½"
    1 rectangle, 9" x 15½"
    1 rectangle, 10" x 15½"
    1 rectangle, 1½" x 4½"

From the multicolored print, cut:
4 strips, 2¼" x 42"

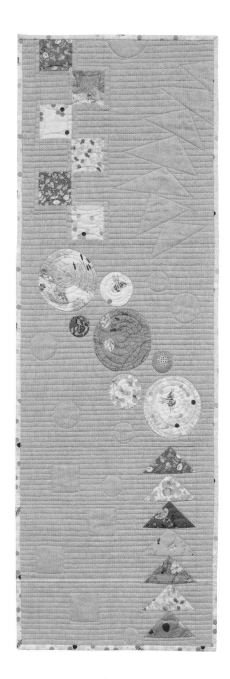

MAKING THE FLYING GEESE BLOCK

1. Using a fabric-marking pen, draw a diagonal line from corner to corner on the wrong side of each linen or beige 2½" square. Place a marked square on one end of a print rectangle, right sides together. Sew along the marked line and trim away the corner fabric, leaving a ¼" seam allowance. Press the seam allowances toward the resulting linen triangle. In the same way, sew a linen square to the other end of the rectangle to complete a flying-geese unit. Make a total of seven units.

Make 7.

2. Sew the flying-geese units together, making sure to orient all the points in the same direction. Sew the linen 1½" x 4½" rectangle to the bottom of the flying-geese strip. Press the seam allowances in the directions indicated. Sew a linen 2" x 15½" rectangle to the right side of the strip. Sew the linen 10" x 15½" rectangle to the left side of the strip to complete the Flying Geese block. Press the seam allowances toward the linen rectangles.

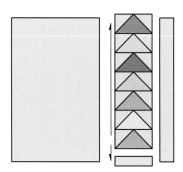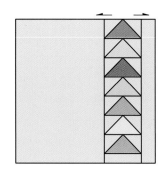

MAKING THE CIRCLES BLOCK

1. Place a print C circle right side down on the *fusible side* of the interfacing. Stitching ¼" inside the raw edge, sew around the circle, slightly overlapping the stitching at the beginning and end of the seam. Trim the excess interfacing even with the raw edges of the circle. Then use pinking shears to trim the seam allowances or use scissors to cut small notches, taking care not to cut into

the stitched line. Make a total of three C circles. In the same manner, make two A circles and two B circles.

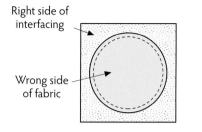

Right side of interfacing

Wrong side of fabric

2. Pinch the interfacing away from a print circle. Carefully cut a small slit in the middle of the interfacing, just large enough to turn the circle through. Turn the circle right side out through the slit. Finger-press the seam allowance, rolling the interfacing to the wrong side of the circle. *Do not use an iron at this point.* In the same way, prepare the remaining circles for appliqué.

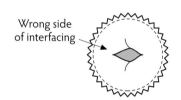

Wrong side of interfacing

3. Place the linen 16" square on a pressing surface. Using the circle placement diagram as a guide, arrange the circle appliqués diagonally across the linen square. Following the manufacturer's instructions, fuse the circles in place.

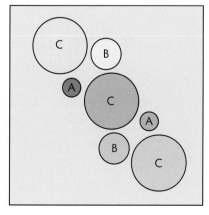

Circle placement

4. Hand or machine stitch around the circles using a blind hem, blanket, zigzag, or straight stitch. Trim the block to measure 15½" square.

MAKING THE TWO-PATCH BLOCK

1. Sew a print square and a linen 3" square right sides together. Press the seam allowances toward the print square. Make a total of six units.

Make 6.

Lock Them Up

Use seam allowances pressed in opposite directions to your advantage and achieve pointy points! Where opposing seam allowances meet, nestle them together tightly and pin through the seam allowances, on both sides of the seam. When sewing the units together, stop with the needle down in the seam allowance and remove the first pin before sewing over it. Continue sewing two or three more stitches and stop again just on the other side of the seam. Remove the second pin before sewing over it. Fine patchwork pins do the best job here.

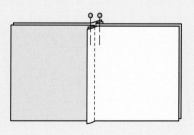

2. Sew the two-patch units together along their long edges, alternating the print and linen squares to form a checkerboard pattern. (See "Lock Them Up" on page 75.) Press the seam allowances open. Sew the remaining linen 2" x 15½" rectangle to one side of the two-patch strip. Sew the linen 9" x 15½" rectangle to the other side of the strip to complete the block. Press the seam allowances toward the rectangles.

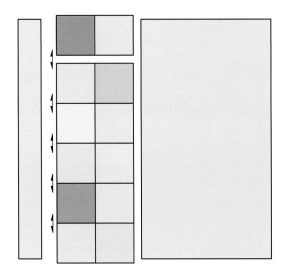

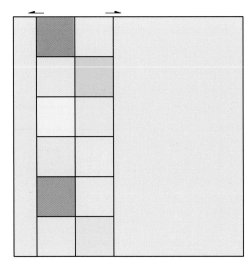

ASSEMBLING THE TABLE RUNNER

Referring to the assembly diagram, arrange the blocks as shown, making sure to orient the shapes so that the diagonal line of circles connects the Flying Geese and Two-Patch blocks, resembling a path of stepping stones along the length of the table runner. Sew the blocks together. Press the seam allowances toward the circle block.

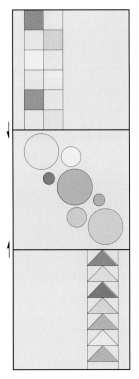

Table-runner assembly

FINISHING THE TABLE RUNNER

For more information on finishing techniques, go to ShopMartingale.com/HowtoQuilt for free illustrated instructions.

1. Layer the table-runner top, batting, and backing; baste the layers together using your favorite method. Quilt as desired. Refer to Krista Withers's "Quilting With Ghost Shapes" on page 78 for quilt design and marking tips specific to this project.

2. Use the multicolored strips to bind the quilt. Add a label (if desired).

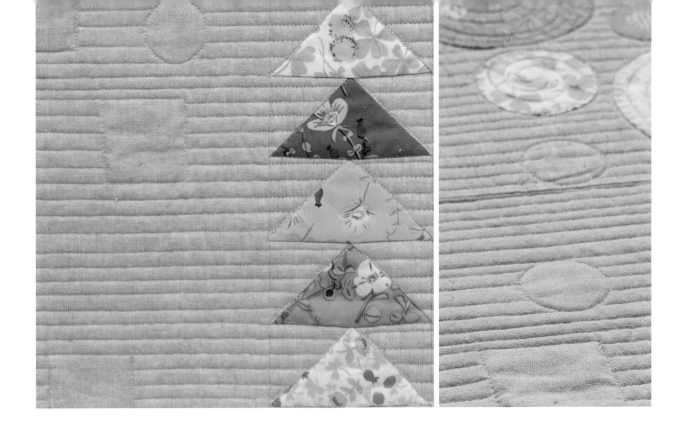

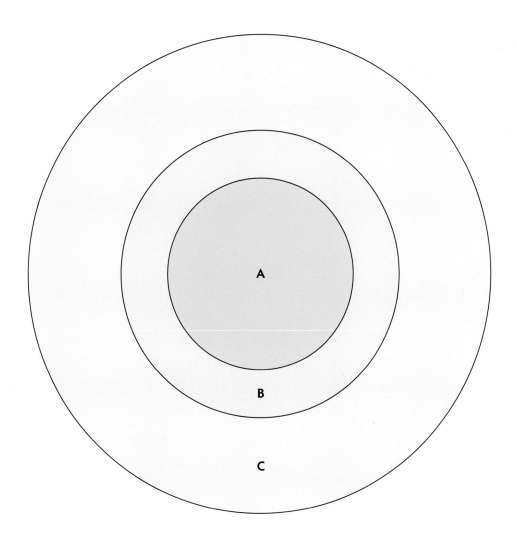

A

B

C

Quilting with Ghost Shapes

Quilting shapes that echo the piecing in a quilt top will add interest and continuity to the overall quilting design. You can quilt a ghost shape of virtually any piecing in your quilt. The pieced elements of your quilt are a great place to look when trying to decide how to quilt the background, or negative space, surrounding the piecing. You can echo quilt the piecing exactly, or take inspiration from small geometric elements in the piecing and quilt them as ghost shapes. For the "Stepping Stones Table Runner" (page 72), I worked with circles, squares, and triangles as ghost shapes.

Krista Withers; photo by Susan Tamcsin

To start, I always audition the designs. Drawing in a sketchbook is a great place to explore ideas, but to really plan the density of quilting, size of shapes, and see how the designs will actually look on your quilt, there's no better tool than a sheet of clear Plexiglas. I use a 20" x 30" sheet, which can be purchased from a home-improvement store. This is a nice size to see quilting scale, even on a larger quilt top. Tape around the perimeter of your Plexiglas with colored painter's tape; this will help prevent you from drawing off the edge and onto your quilt. Please learn from my mistake and do this simple step! I use a wet-erase marker when drawing, but a dry-erase marker will work as well. Beware that both markers *will* stain your quilt, so take care when using this marker and try to always draw on the same side of the Plexiglass sheet.

1. Lay the Plexiglas over your quilt top on a large, flat surface.

2. Start by marking your ghost shapes. Play with the direction or orientation, the scale, and the placement of the shapes in the negative space. Try reversing the direction or use a mirror image. Enjoy this process—the fewer rules you give yourself at this point the greater chance you have of finding a design that is uniquely you.

3. Nothing is set in stone so don't be critical of your drawing. This is a tool that's there to help you. If you don't like your design, erase it and start over! Try to match the scale of your ghost shapes to the scale of the piecing to maintain continuity in the overall quilt design.

4. Once you like the placement of your shapes, start auditioning background fill patterns. For this project, I used straight lines spaced about ½" apart. Keep in mind the density of your quilting. Try to maintain a consistent density of quilting lines over the surface of the quilt to avoid distortion and warping in your finished piece. If you're an experienced free-motion quilter, feel free to draw in swirls, paisleys, meandering lines, or any other continuous-line design you feel comfortable with. If you're new to machine quilting, you may want to stick with straight lines that you can sew with your walking foot.

When you feel confident with your design on the Plexiglas, you're ready to mark your quilt top.

5. Start by marking the ghost shapes on your quilt top with the marker of choice. My favorite marking tools are a blue water-soluble pen for light-colored fabrics, a white wax pen for dark-colored fabrics, and a chalk wheel. I only mark the ghost shapes, not the background fill

lines, but you may find it helpful to draw in one straight line as a starting point. Use the edge of your presser foot or a seam guide arm to maintain consistent spacing as you sew lines parallel to the marked one.

6. After basting the quilt top, batting, and backing, quilt the ghost circles by carefully following the drawn line. Then quilt the ghost squares. Referring to the diagram, quilt the ghost geese in a continuous line starting at the top triangle point. Zigzag your way down the left side of all the triangles, across the base of the bottom triangle, and then back up the right side. Try to meet all of the points.

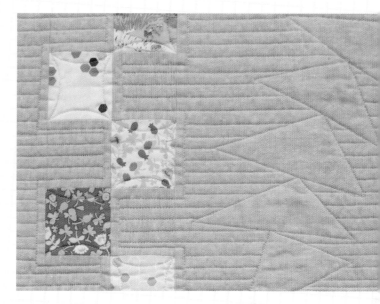

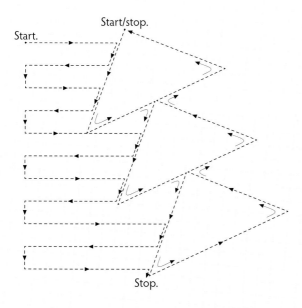

7. Once the ghost shapes are quilted, sew horizontal lines, ½" apart. Start at the edge of the quilt and sew to the edge of the ghost shape. Turn the quilt and stitch exactly on top of the ghost-shape line for ½"; then turn the quilt and sew parallel to the first straight line in the opposite direction. When you reach the edge of the quilt, turn again and sew ½" along the edge of the quilt. Turn back toward your ghost shape. Because there will be a fair amount of back tracking (sewing on top

of previously stitched lines) I use a neutral-colored 50-weight thread to reduce thread build up.

NOTE: If you use free-motion quilting instead of straight lines, quilt right up to the ghost designs, backtrack a little, and then continue filling the negative space with your continuous line design. By quilting right up to the ghost shapes and doing a little backtracking, you'll give the shapes a bit of poof.

8. If you'd like to add some quilting inside the pieced motifs, try a swirl in the larger circles and a gentle curve inside the two-patch squares. The narrow table runner makes it fairly manageable to turn the work in a domestic machine, so try the swirls with a walking foot and a slow speed setting.

Inventing quilting designs doesn't have to be difficult. Look to your quilt top for inspiration and keep it simple. Drawing on Plexiglas gives you a lot of freedom to explore ideas and audition quilting designs in true scale. Remember to enjoy the process; the more you practice, the easier it will be to quilt your own projects with confidence.

Woven Place Mats

FINISHED SIZE: 25½" (at widest point) x 14"

Designed and made by Felicity Ronaghan

These cheerful place mats are the perfect project to use up your scrappy strips. Felicity's clever no-piecing-required project makes use of fusible woven interfacing to secure the woven fabric strips prior to topstitching. Make two place mats at a time by first creating a woven semi-circle, then cutting it in half for two place mats! Four of these place mats fit perfectly around a 36" diameter table.

MATERIALS

Yardage is based on 42"-wide fabric unless otherwise noted.
Yields 4 place mats.

25 strips, 1½" x various lengths 20" to 42", of assorted light prints
25 strips, 1½" x various lengths 20" to 42", of assorted dark prints
1¼ yards of fabric for backing
1 yard *total* of black prints for binding
2¼ yards of 20"-wide lightweight, woven fusible interfacing
2 pieces, 20" x 40", of batting
20" x 36" piece of craft paper
Yardstick compass (optional)
Removable fabric-marking pen or chalk
Thick permanent marker
Glue stick (optional)

CUTTING

All measurements include a ¼" seam allowance unless otherwise noted.

From the interfacing, cut:
2 rectangles, 20" x 39"

From the black prints, cut:
2¼"-wide *bias* strips to total 270"

From the backing fabric, cut:
2 rectangles, 21" x 40"

MAKING THE PAPER TEMPLATE

1. Fold the paper in half along the 36" edge and crease the fold. Using a long ruler, measure 18" up from the bottom edge and mark a dot on the fold.

2. Angle the top of the ruler about an inch away from the first dot, leaving the bottom of the ruler at the base of the fold. Make another dot at 18". Continue marking various dots along an arc, always measuring 18" from the base of the fold. Freehand draw a curved line to join the dots. Or, use a yardstick compass (or a pencil tied to a piece of string) to draw an 18" arc.

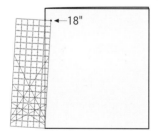
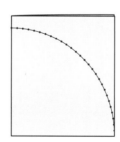

3. Cut out the quarter-circle along the drawn arc. Open the paper out flat to make a half-circle. Using the permanent marker, draw a thick, dark line along the fold.

MAKING THE PLACE MATS

1. Fold one rectangle of interfacing in half along the long edge. Refold the paper template in half and place it on top of the interfacing, aligning the folds and straight bottom edges. Using the paper template as a guide, cut the interfacing approximately 1½" beyond the edge of the template.

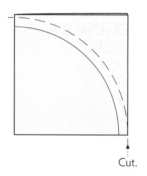
Cut.
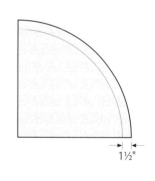
1½"

2. Unfold the paper template to make a half-circle and place it on a heat-resistant surface with the drawn line facing up. Unfold the interfacing and center it on top of the paper template with the bottom edges aligned

and the *fusible side* facing up. Make sure the interfacing completely covers the template. Secure the two layers in place using a bit of glue stick, if desired.

3. Separate the assorted strips into two sets, one with light prints and one with dark prints. Decide which set of strips will be placed horizontally; the second set of strips will be placed vertically.

4. Select a strip at least 40" long and place it horizontally along the bottom edge of the interfacing base, right side up. Make sure the strip reaches the left and right edges of the interfacing. If more than one strip is needed to reach the 40" length, simply overlap the ends of two adjoining strips by 2".

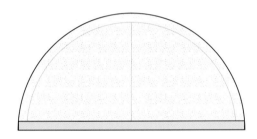

5. Continue laying out strips, butting the horizontal raw edges up to the previous strip, until the interfacing is fully covered. Do not overlap the long, horizontal edges of the strips. Make use of shorter strips as you move up the semi-circle.

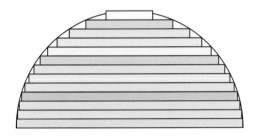

6. Now it's time to start weaving. Fold the bottom strip halfway back onto itself until the center line on the paper template is visible through

the interfacing. In the same way, fold back *every other* horizontal strip.

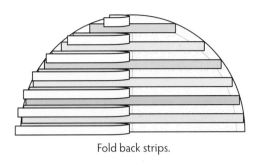

Fold back strips.

7. Choose a strip from your second set of strips that's at least 20" long. Place it vertically, on top of the unfolded horizontal strips. Align the left edge of the strip with the marked line on the paper template.

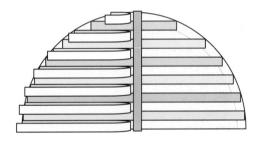

8. Unfold all of the horizontal strips so they are laying flat across the interfacing base. Beginning with the second horizontal strip from the bottom, fold back every other strip until it meets the vertical strip.

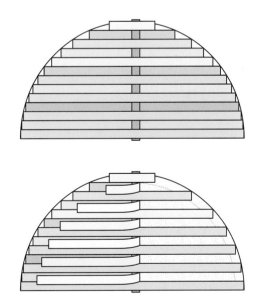

10. Repeat steps 6–9, gradually using shorter strips as required, until the right side of the interfacing half-circle is fully covered.

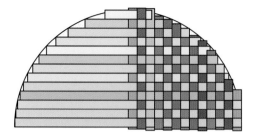

11. Beginning again at the center and moving to the left, repeat steps 6–9 until the entire half-circle is covered in woven strips.

12. Following the manufacturer's instructions, fuse the woven strips to the interfacing. *Do not* trim the place mat yet. Carefully remove the paper template from the back of the place mat and save for trimming later.

13. Repeat steps 1–12 to make a second woven half-circle.

FINISHING THE PLACE MATS

For more information on finishing techniques, go to www.ShopMartingale.com/HowtoQuilt for free illustrated instructions.

1. Layer each woven half-circle with batting and backing, making sure there's at least 1" of batting beyond the straight bottom edge of the half-circle. Baste the layers together using your preferred method. *NOTE*: if using safety pins, place them in the middle of the squares.

2. To quilt each half-circle, set your machine to a regular zigzag stitch. Beginning with the center vertical strip, align the middle of your presser foot with the edge of the strip and zigzag stitch along the edge of the strip. You will be stitching down the raw edges and quilting the woven half-circle at the same time. Zigzag stitch all of the horizontal and vertical strip edges.

9. Lay the second vertical strip on top of the horizontal strips, butting the left edge against the right edge of the first vertical strip. Unfold all of the horizontal strips so they're flat again. You should see the beginning of a light/dark checkerboard pattern emerging.

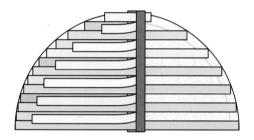

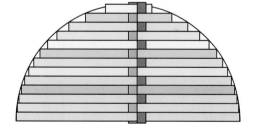

3. Using a rotary cutter and ruler, trim the straight edge of a half-circle along the bottom edge of the bottom horizontal strip. Place the half-circle paper template on top of the quilted half-circle, aligning the straight bottom edges and the vertical center line. Pin through the paper template in a few places to secure it. Trace around the template with a fabric-marking pen. Cut out a half-circle on the drawn line. Repeat to trim the second half-circle.

4. Cut vertically through the center of the half-circle, yielding two quarter-circles. In the corner of each quarter-circle, measure 4½" from the corner as shown. Use a compass to draw an arc, and then trim along the drawn line. Repeat to make a total of four place mats.

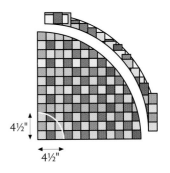

5. Use the bias strips to bind each place mat. It's easiest to join the ends of the binding along a straight edge of the place mat rather than on the curved edge.

Felicity Ronaghan

One morning, I asked my six-year-old daughter what she thought I liked best about quilting retreats, she replied without one moment's hesitation: "Quiet time to sew!" She's right of course, but there's much more to it than that. Whether it is a one-day retreat in a community hall or a multi-night stay at a conference center, it's the concentrated time to spend on something I truly love that feeds my soul. My usual 20-minute stints at my machine during any given evening are just top-ups to my tank; going on retreat is like the full engine overhaul plus the deluxe detailing.

At the end of our conversation, my daughter added, "I know what you like least about quilting retreats: missing your family!" And she's right about that too. I return home from my retreats not exhausted but energized, my soul newly nourished, my mind bursting with creativity, my tank full to overflowing.

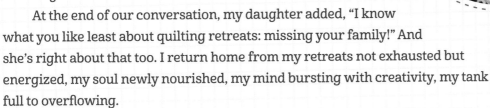

Lone Star Circle Quilt

FINISHED SIZE: 55½" x 55½"

Designed and made by Lynne Goldsworthy featuring Oakshott Lipari and Impressions shot cottons on a background print from Aspen Frost by Basic Grey for Moda

Lynne has adapted a favorite traditional quilt pattern, the Lone Star, to create this circle variation using colors reminiscent of twentieth-century Amish quilts. Use it as a lap quilt or a generous-sized wall hanging.

MATERIALS

Yardage is based on 42"-wide fabric unless otherwise noted.

¼ yard *each* of 18 assorted dark shot cottons for diamonds and binding*

⅛ yard *each* of 12 assorted light shot cottons for diamonds*

2⅛ yards of cream print for background

3½ yards of fabric for backing

60" x 60" piece of batting

*A shot cotton *uses one thread color for the warp and a different thread color for the weft, giving the fabric depth and visual interest. If you prefer, you can substitute a solid fabric.*

CUTTING

All measurements include a ¼" seam allowance unless otherwise noted.

From the cream print, cut:
8 strips, 3½" x 42"
2 squares, 15" x 15"; cut in half diagonally to yield 4 triangles
6 strips, 4½" x 42"

From *each* of the light and dark shot cottons, cut:
1 strip, 3½" x 42" (30 total)

From *each* of 12 dark shot cottons, cut:
1 strip, 2¼" x 21" (12 total)

MAKING THE STRIP SETS

1. Sew the cream 3½"-wide strips end to end. Cut the pieced strip into 12 strips, 25" long.

2. Trim each shot cotton 3½"-wide strip to measure 25" long.

3. Using the 25"-long dark shot cotton, light shot cotton, and cream strips and offsetting the ends of the strips approximately 3" as shown, join the strips along their long edges to make strip sets as indicated below.

   Set 1: dark, light, dark, light, dark, and cream. Press the seam allowances toward the cream strip. Make two.

   Set 2: light, dark, light, dark, and cream. Press the seam allowances away from the cream strip. Make two.

   Set 3: dark, light, dark, and cream. Press the seam allowances toward the cream strip. Make two.

   Set 4: light, dark, and cream. Press the seam allowances away from the cream strip. Make two.

   Set 5: dark and cream. Press the seam allowances toward the cream strip. Make two.

   Two cream strips will be left over. These will be cut into individual diamonds.

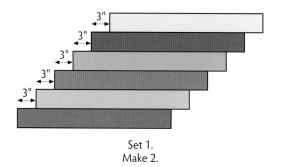

Set 1.
Make 2.

4. Using a rotary cutter and a ruler with 45° markings, align the 45° line with the seam line on a strip set as shown. Trim off the irregular ends of the strip set. Rotate the strip set 180°. Measure 3½" from the freshly cut end of the strip set and cut a 3½"-wide segment. Cut a total of four segments.

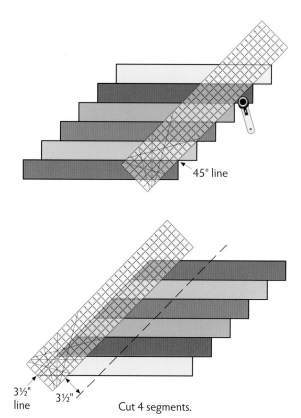

45° line

3½" line   3½"   Cut 4 segments.

5. Repeat step 4 to cut four segments from each of the remaining strip sets. The segments have been cut on the bias, so handle them with care. Try not to fold the strips for storage; instead, lay them flat on a work surface.

6. Layer the two remaining cream strips, carefully matching the raw edges. In the same manner, cut a total of eight diamonds.

MAKING THE LONE STAR BLOCK

1. Lay out one of each segment as shown. Sew the segments together to make a wedge shape. Take care to match the points where intersecting seams meet; see "Matching Points on Angled Seams" at right. Press the seam allowances open. Make eight wedges.

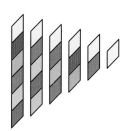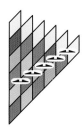

Wedge assembly.
Make 8.

2. Sew two wedges together to make a quarter-circle. Press the seam allowances open. Make four.

Make 4.

3. Sew two quarter-circles together to make a half-circle. Press the seam allowances open. Make two.

Make 2.

4. Sew the half-circles together to complete the Lone Star block. Press the seam allowances open.

Matching Points on Angled Seams

When angled seams are placed right sides together they do not line up like straight seams do, so it's not possible to "lock" seam allowances for accuracy. For this project, lay two segments right sides up as shown in the wedge assembly diagram at left. Flip the segment on the right on top of the segment on the left, right sides together. At each seam, insert a fine straight pin through the seam ¼" from the raw edge of the segment. Make sure the pin emerges exactly on the seam of the bottom segment. If not, adjust the strips until the pin goes exactly through both seams and is ¼" from the raw edges. While this pin is sticking perpendicular through the two points to be matched, place a second straight pin just before the seam intersection and a third pin just after the seam intersection. Remove the middle pin and sew the segments together using a ¼"-wide seam allowance.

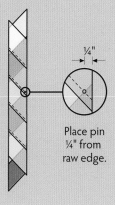

¼"

Place pin
¼" from
raw edge.

COMPLETING THE QUILT TOP

1. Align the ¼" line on a ruler with the outer points of the dark diamonds. Trim away the excess cream fabric across the top of each wedge segment as shown.

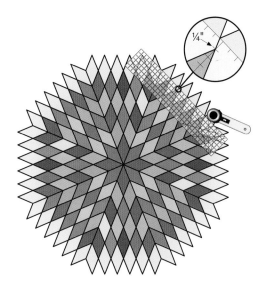

2. Fold each cream triangle in half and finger-press to mark the center of the long side. Sew a cream triangle to one corner of the Lone Star circle, matching the center crease to the midpoint on the corner wedge. Press the seam allowances toward the cream triangle. In the same way, sew cream triangles to the three remaining corners of the Lone Star circle. Trim and square up the cream triangles. The quilt-top center should measure 47½" x 47½".

3. Sew the cream 4½"-wide strips end to end. From the pieced strip, cut two 47½"-long strips and two 55½"-long strips. Sew the 47½"-long strip to opposite sides of the quilt-top center. Press seam allowances toward the cream strips. Sew the 55½"-long strips to the top and bottom of the quilt top. Press the seam allowances toward the cream strips.

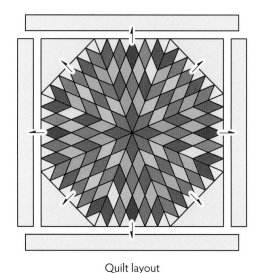

Quilt layout

FINISHING THE QUILT

For more information on finishing techniques, go to ShopMartingale.com/HowtoQuilt for free illustrated instructions.

1. Cut the backing fabric into two equal lengths and remove the selvage edges. Sew the lengths together using a ½" seam allowance. Press the seam allowances open.

2. Layer the quilt top, batting, and backing; baste the layers together using your preferred method. Quilt as desired. The sample quilt is quilted using straight lines 1" apart following some of the seams in the quilt top.

3. Trim the backing and batting to even with the quilt top.

4. Use the dark 2¼"-wide strips to bind the quilt. Add a label and hanging sleeve (if desired).

Lynne Goldsworthy

Each year, two friends and I run a modern-quilting retreat over a July weekend in London, England. Although we always look for great teachers and interesting workshops, we've come to realize that the most important and fun thing about the weekend is spending time with other quilters. In previous years, we each taught several workshops and spent the rest of our time actually running the retreat—moving sewing machines, irons, ironing boards, and tables around the venue, or setting up rooms for the next workshop, lunch, or presentation.

This year, realizing we didn't have to do it all ourselves, we made a change. We taught as little as possible and brought in my teenage son and his friend to do all of the heavy lifting. We were able to spend more time stitching and socializing with the retreat attendees and that really made this year the most special for us.

Orange Grove Quilt

FINISHED QUILT: 71½" x 71½" • FINISHED BLOCK: 10" x 10"

Designed and made by Krista Hennebury and quilted by Krista Withers

A modern take on the classic Pine Tree block, "Orange Grove Quilt" is a fresh-squeezed update featuring a combination of aqua and orange. Solid alternating blocks and large corner setting triangles provide lots of negative space to explore quilting options. Consider making an apple orchard with red prints or a citrus grove with yellow, green, and orange fabrics! Chain piecing the half-square triangles will speed up your block production so that you could complete this quilt top on a weekend retreat.

MATERIALS

Yardage is based on 42"-wide fabric unless otherwise noted.

4¾ yards of white solid for blocks and background
13 fat eighths (9" x 21") of assorted orange prints for blocks*
13 scraps, at least 4" x 4", of aqua prints for blocks
⅝ yard of orange print for binding
4½ yards of fabric for backing
77" x 77" piece of batting

Choose a mix of light, medium, and dark prints.

CUTTING

All measurements include a ¼" seam allowance unless otherwise noted.

From the white solid, cut:
2 squares, 37" x 37"; cut in half diagonally to yield 4 triangles*
4 strips, 10½" x 42"; crosscut into 12 squares, 10½" x 10½"
1 strip, 5¼" x 42"; crosscut into 7 squares, 5¼" x 5¼". Cut the squares
    into quarters diagonally to yield 28 triangles (2 will be extra).
8 strips, 3" x 42"; crosscut into 98 squares, 3" x 3". Cut *7 of the squares*
    in half diagonally to yield 14 triangles (1 will be extra).
2 strips, 2½" x 42"; crosscut into 26 squares, 2½" x 2½"

See "Bias Edges" on page 94.

From *each* orange fat eighth, cut:
1 square, 6⅞" x 6⅞"; cut in half diagonally to yield 2 triangles
    (26 total; 13 will be extra)
7 squares, 3" x 3" (91 total)

From *each* aqua print, cut:
1 square, 3⅜" x 3⅜" (13 total)

From the orange print for binding, cut:
8 strips, 2¼" x 42"

Bias Edges

Wait to cut the large white triangles until you're ready to attach them to the quilt top. Long bias edges are prone to stretching, so it's best not to handle them too much or fold them up for storage. To mark the diagonal cut, fold the white 37" square in half diagonally. Spray the fold with starch and press with vertical up and down movements of your iron. Open the square on your cutting mat and cut along the crease using a long ruler and rotary cutter.

MAKING THE BLOCKS

1. Mark a diagonal line from corner to corner on the wrong side of each white 3" square. Layer a marked square right sides together with an orange square. Sew ¼" from each side of the marked line. Cut the squares apart on the marked line to make two half-square-triangle units. Press the seam allowances toward the orange triangle. Trim the unit to measure 2½" x 2½". Make a total of 182 units.

Make 182.

2. Using 14 matching half-square-triangle units and two white 2½" squares, join the pieces into rows to make three units as shown. Press the seam allowances as indicated to create opposing seams. This will help lock the seams during block construction.

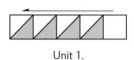

Unit 1.

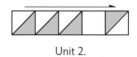

Unit 2.

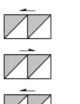 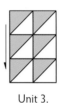

Unit 3.

3. Sew white 5¼" triangles to opposite sides of an aqua square as shown. Press the seam allowances toward the aqua square. Sew a white 3" triangle to the bottom of the aqua square to make a base unit. Press the seam allowances toward the white triangle. Make 13 units.

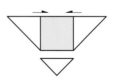 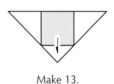

Make 13.

4. Choose an orange triangle that contrasts with the print in the half-square-triangle units. Fold the orange triangle in half and finger-press to mark the center of the long side. Fold the aqua square in half and finger-press. Sew the triangle to the top of the aqua unit, matching the center creases. Press the seam allowances

toward the orange triangle. Make 13 units. (You'll have 1 extra triangle from each orange print to use in another project.)

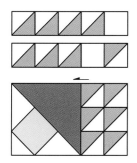

Match creases.

Make 13.

5. Sew the units together as shown to complete a Tree block. Press the seam allowances in the directions indicated. Make a total of 13 blocks.

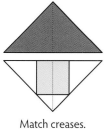 

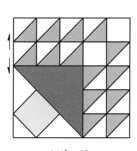

Make 13.

ASSEMBLING THE QUILT TOP

1. Lay out the Tree blocks and white 10½" squares in five rows, alternating the blocks and squares as shown in the row assembly diagram. Join the blocks and squares into rows. Press the seam allowances toward the white squares. Join the rows and press the seam allowances open to reduce bulk.

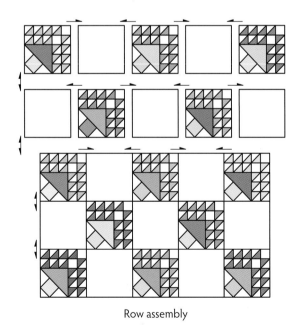

Row assembly

2. Fold each white 37" triangle in half and finger-press to mark the center of the long side. Fold the quilt top in half vertically and horizontally; finger-press to mark the center on each side. Sew a white triangle to each side of the quilt top, matching the center creases. Press the seam allowances toward the white triangles.

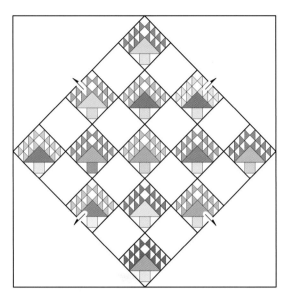

Quilt layout

FINISHING THE QUILT

For more information on finishing techniques, go to ShopMartingale.com/HowtoQuilt for free illustrated instructions.

1. Cut the backing fabric into two equal lengths and remove the selvage edges. Sew the lengths together using a ½" seam allowance. Press the seam allowances open.

2. Layer the quilt top, batting, and backing; baste the layers together using your preferred method. Quilt as desired. The sample was custom quilted by Krista Withers using her signature Ghost Quilting designs (see page 78)—in this case, straight lines and swirling filler motifs.

3. Trim the backing and batting even with the quilt top.

4. Use the orange 2¼"-wide strips to bind the quilt. Add a label and hanging sleeve (if desired).

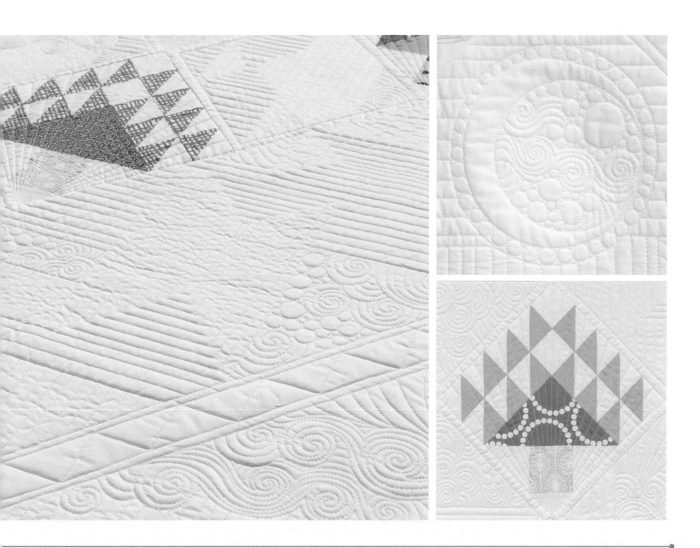

Machine Quilting

Krista Withers worked her long-arm magic on "Orange Grove Quilt" with very little direction from me. The only specific quilting I requested was one of her signature moons (shown above, top right). Krista's treatment of this quilt is a very modern one—instead of quilting to highlight the piecing, she quilted to highlight the negative space, creating interest where there was only a blank square or triangle of white fabric. Ghost shapes of the pieced triangles are included in the quilting to provide continuity in the quilt's overall design, while filler motifs of intersecting straight lines, bubbles, spirals, and square mazes add so much interest.

Krista outlined the alternate white blocks with a frame of straight stitching, and then quilted a unique free-motion composition within each block, while quilting every tree block with the same fan. This juxtaposition is very effective and gives the quilt an energy that keeps your eye moving. Every bit of negative space has its own unique quilted story! To find out more about Krista's designs, check out "Contributors" on page 109.

Macaron Delight Quilt

FINISHED QUILT: 47½" x 62" • FINISHED STRIP: 7½" x 53½"

Designed, pieced, and quilted by Christina Lane

Cheerful pastel colors in the distinctive shape of delectable French meringue cookies inspired the name of this quilt. Don't be put off at the prospect of piecing this quilt; curved piecing is not nearly as challenging as you might think. The macaron shapes in this quilt have more gentle curves than the quarter-circles commonly used in traditional curved blocks .

MATERIALS

Yardage is based on 42"-wide fabric unless otherwise noted.

3⅜ yards of white solid for background, sashing, and borders
12 fat eighths (9" x 21") of assorted prints for *macarons*
½ yard of gold print for binding
3¼ yards of fabric for backing
53" x 67" piece of batting
Heavyweight template plastic
Fine-point permanent pen
Removable fabric-marking pen or chalk
18 mm rotary cutter (optional)

CUTTING

All measurements include a ¼" seam allowance unless otherwise noted.

From the *lengthwise grain* of the white solid, cut:
2 strips, 42" x 54"; crosscut into:
    4 strips, 8" x 54"
    4 strips, 4½" x 54"
    3 strips, 3½" x 54"

From *each* assorted print, cut:
1 strip, 4" x 18" (12 total)

From the gold print, cut:
6 strips, 2¼" x 42"

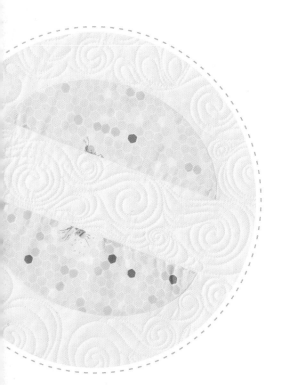

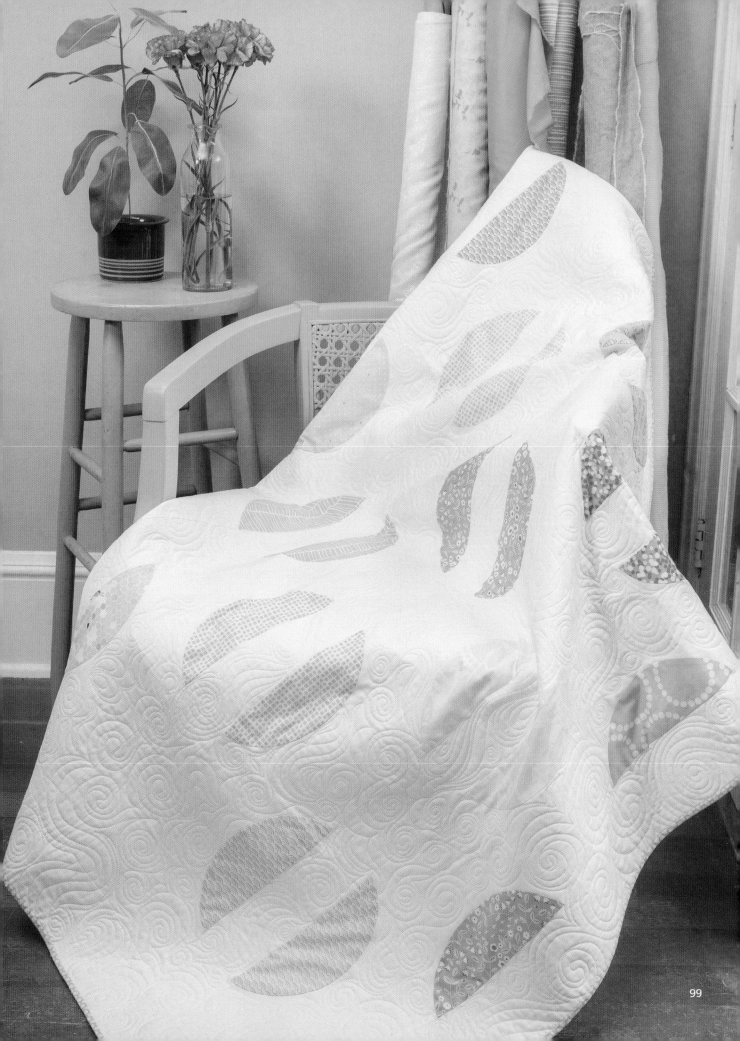

2. Using a fabric-marking pen, mark one of the white 8"-wide strips as follows. Starting on the left edge, measure down 6¼" from the top of the strip and make a mark. Measure 15½" from the first mark and make another mark. Measure 15½" from the second mark and make a third mark. On the right edge of the same strip, measure down 14" from the top and make a mark. Measure 15½" from the first mark and make another mark. Measure 15½" from the second mark and make a third mark. Label as strip A. Repeat to mark a second identical A strip.

3. The B strips are a mirror image of the A strips. Mark each remaining white 8"-wide strip as follows. Starting on the left edge, measure down 14" from the top of the strip and make a mark; measure down 15½" and make a second mark; and then measure down 15½" and make a third mark. On the right edge of each strip, measure down 6¼" from the top and make a mark; measure down 15½" and make a second mark; and then measure down 15½" and make a third mark.

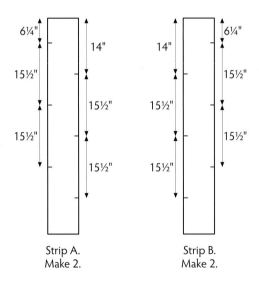

Strip A.
Make 2.

Strip B.
Make 2.

Macaron vs. Macaroon

Macaron (pronounced mah-kah-ROHN) is the French word for two petite, round, and colorful meringue cookies that sandwich a layer of buttercream or ganache between them—not to be confused with the chewy coconut, sugar, and egg confection commonly known as a macaroon *in North America.*

PREPARING THE BACKGROUND STRIPS AND *MACARON* SHAPES

1. To make templates, trace the outer lines of the A and B patterns (page 103) onto template plastic using a fine-point permanent pen, making sure to trace the lines exactly. Cut out the templates, cutting exactly on the drawn lines. The inner line of the templates indicates the sewing line.

4. Fold one A strip so that all of the markings on the left edge are exactly on top of each other. Pin the layers together so that they don't shift. With the curved edge toward the outer edge of the strip, place template A on the folded strip

and align the center line on the template with the marks on the strip. Using an 18 mm rotary cutter or scissors, cut along the curved edge *only*, cutting through all the layers. Unfold the strip. Repeat the process on the right edge of the same strip. Place a pin at the top of the strip to remind you which way is "up."

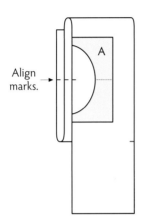

Align marks.

5. Repeat step 4 using the remaining A strip and the two B strips.

6. Layer two print strips on top of each other, carefully aligning all of the raw edges. Place template B at one end, with the straight edge of the template exactly on the long edge of the strips. Cut along the curved edge to make two *macaron* shapes. Flip the template so that the straight edge is aligned with the opposite edge of the strips and cut two more *macaron* shapes. If you *don't* have a ¼" presser foot, mark the sewing line on the wrong side of the fabric B shapes using a removable fabric-marking pen. Cut a total of 24 *macaron* shapes.

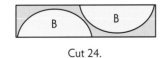

Cut 24.

SEWING THE CURVES

1. Refer to the quilt photo (page 100) and quilt assembly diagram (page 102) as needed. On a design wall or other flat surface arrange the *macaron* shapes on the A and B strips,

placing the like-fabric shapes opposite each other to create the *macarons*. Rearrange the shapes until you're satisfied with the layout. Starting at the top of an A strip, sew the top-left *macaron* shape to the strip, referring to "New to Curves?," above right, as needed.

2. Sew the next *macaron* on the right edge of the strip. Continue sewing *macaron* shapes to the A strip, alternating the left and right sides of the strip as you work down the strip. In the same way, sew *macaron* shapes to the second A strip.

New to Curves?

Before tackling a full strip of macarons, *make a single one using scraps to practice pinning and sewing a smooth curve with a ¼" seam allowance. Using the same templates as the quilt, cut one* macaron *B shape from a scrap 4" x 9" rectangle and one background A shape from a scrap 8" x 14" rectangle. Fold each piece in half and finger-press the center point on the curves. With right sides together, match the two center creases and pin. Then match the top and bottom edges of the curves and pin. Ease the curved, raw edges together and pin along the curved edge to hold everything in place. If you have the following features on your machine, set the speed to slow, the needle position to needle down, and engage the dual feed. With the* macaron *fabric on top, start sewing from one end of the curve. Stop and remove each pin before sewing over it! Press the seam allowances toward the* macaron.

3. Repeat steps 1 and 2, sewing *macaron* shapes to each B strip.

ASSEMBLING THE QUILT TOP

1. Referring to the quilt layout at right, lay out the white 3½"-wide strips and the A and B strips, making sure the like-fabric shapes are across from each other as shown. Pin and sew the strips together, carefully matching the centers of the *macaron* pairs across from each other. The quilt top should measure 39½" x 54".

2. Sew white 4½"-long strips to opposite sides of the quilt-top center. Press the seam allowances toward the white strips.

3. Measure the width of the quilt top across the center, including the just-added borders. Trim the two remaining white 4½"-wide strips to this length. Sew the strips to the top and bottom of the quilt top to complete the border. Press the seam allowances toward the white strips.

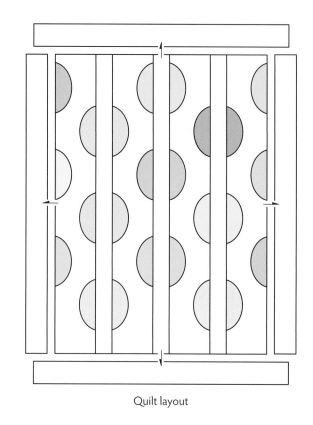

Quilt layout

Christina Lane

I firmly believe that to truly take a break, I have to leave home behind. If I don't have my computer with me, I'm forced to take a break from work. A sewing retreat is the perfect excuse to take time off and actually create.

More than just the time spent sewing at a retreat, I love the interaction with like-minded people, where I can talk about fat quarters and ¼" seam allowances and not have to explain myself. We talk about our families and our struggle to fit creativity into each day. I also find these events allow me to really bond with my sewing friends. When you spend evenings in pj's talking about whatever comes up, you find a deeper connection to the people you've already befriended online. You find out how much you really have in common and are able to open up in a whole new way.

FINISHING THE QUILT

For more information on finishing techniques, go to ShopMartingale.com/HowtoQuilt for free illustrated instructions.

1. Cut the backing fabric into two equal lengths and remove the selvage edges. Sew the lengths together using a ½" seam allowance. Press the seam allowances open.

2. Layer the quilt top, batting, and backing; baste the layers together using your preferred method. Quilt as desired. The sample quilt is quilted in an allover, swirling, continuous-line design in the background fabric only. This quilting design leaves the *macarons* soft and slightly raised from the background.

3. Trim the backing and batting even with the quilt top.

4. Use the gold 2¼"-wide strips to bind the quilt. Add a label and hanging sleeve (if desired).

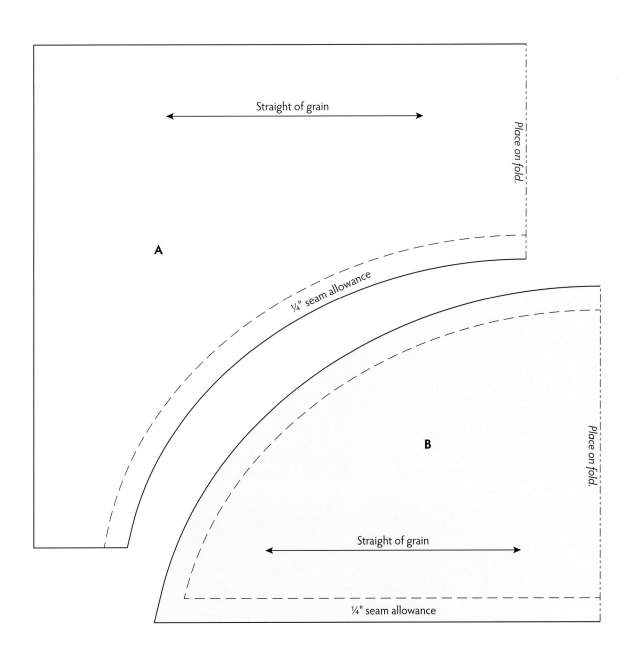

Straight of grain

Place on fold.

A

¼" seam allowance

Place on fold.

B

Straight of grain

¼" seam allowance

Rainbow 'Round the Cabin Quilt

FINISHED SIZE: 48½" x 48½"

Designed and quilted by Krista Hennebury, made with friends

Piecing this Log Cabin quilt is a wonderful afternoon activity for six quilting friends. It's a fun way to create six simple, colorful quilts in the space of a few hours! Each participant chooses one of six rainbow colors and brings 6½"-wide fabric strips representing her color choice to the sew-in. At the end of the afternoon everyone leaves with a lap-sized quilt top. Why not suggest this activity for your guild's next charity sewing event or day retreat?

MATERIALS

Yardage is based on 42"-wide fabric unless otherwise noted. Materials listed are per person, based on 6 participants.

1 quilt block *OR* 1 square of print fabric for Log Cabin center, 12½" x 12½"

2¼ yards *total* of assorted solids or prints for logs*

½ yard of fabric for binding

3¼ yards of fabric for backing

54" x 54" piece of batting

*Prior to the sew-in, each participant chooses one of the following colors to sew with: red, orange, yellow, green, blue, or violet. All strips do not need to be the same solid or print as long as they read as the chosen color. Keep in mind that blue could range from aqua to sky to navy blue. Similarly, red can include pink, fuchsia, or cherry!

CUTTING

All measurements include a ¼" seam allowance unless otherwise noted.

From the assorted solids or prints, cut a *total* of:
11 strips, 6½" x 42"

From the binding fabric, cut:
6 strips, 2¼" x 42"

MAKING THE QUILT TOP

Position quilters around a large dining table or at sewing stations around a room based on their color choice; alternate warm and cool fabric colors. This way, the resulting Log Cabin quilts will have warm colors (yellow, orange, red) on one diagonal and cool colors (green, blue, violet) on the opposite diagonal. Participants always sew with their own fabric strips. Each participant begins sewing with his or her own center block and colored strips.

1. Refer to the quilt layout diagram at right for placement guidance as needed. To add log #1, sew an assorted strip to the right-hand side of the 12½" block or square. Press the seam allowances toward the strip. Trim the strip even with the edge of the center block.

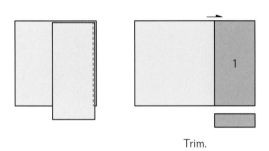

Trim.

2. To add log #2, turn the block 90° counter-clockwise and sew an assorted strip log to the right edge of the center unit. Press the seam allowances toward log #2. Trim the strip even with the edge of the center block.

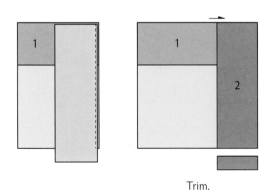

Trim.

3. Pass the center unit to the person on your left and receive a new center unit from the person on your right. Position the center unit so that log #2 is at the bottom. To add log #3, sew an assorted strip log to the left side of the unit. Press the seam allowances toward log #3 and trim as before. In the same way, add log #4, press, and trim.

4. Pass the quilt top to your left again. Continue adding two logs to the quilt top in the same manner. As the Log Cabin grows, you'll have to join some of the trimmed strips end to end to create longer strips. When your center square returns to you, it should be surrounded by two logs each of six different colors. Your quilt top is complete. No two quilts will look exactly alike.

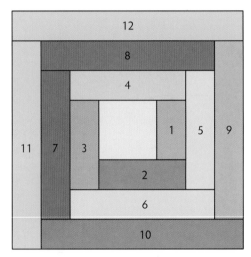

Quilt layout

FINISHING THE QUILT

For more information on finishing techniques, go to ShopMartingale.com/HowtoQuilt for free illustrated instructions.

1. Cut the backing fabric into two equal lengths and remove the selvage edges. Sew the lengths together using a ½" seam allowance. Press the seam allowances open.

2. Layer the quilt top, batting, and backing; baste the layers together using your preferred method. Quilt as desired. Quilting suggestions include an allover free-motion meander or floral motif, horizontal straight lines spaced 1½" apart (see "Straight-Line Quilting" below), or a diagonal grid of straight lines spaced 2" apart.

3. Trim the backing and batting even with the quilt top.

4. Use the 2¼"-wide strips to bind the quilt. Add a label and hanging sleeve (if desired).

Straight-Line Quilting

To temporarily mark straight quilting lines on a quilt top, simply apply a long strip of painter's masking tape directly to your quilt. Regular masking tape can leave glue residue on fabric. Sew adjacent to the edge of the tape, not through the tape. Remove the tape and reapply it for the next line. Remove all of the tape before storing your quilt.

From top to bottom at right: made and quilted by Jo Ann Lee, Felicity Ronaghan, and Andrea Cowie

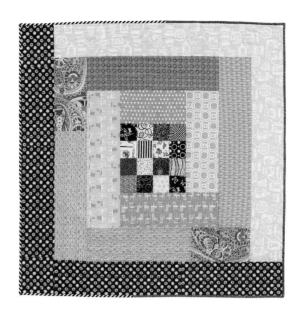

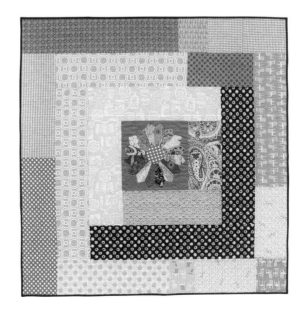

RESOURCES

FABRIC

Cloud 9 organics
cloud9fabrics.com

Oakshott Lipari and
Impressions shot cottons
www.oakshottfabrics.com

Basic Grey for Moda
unitednotions.com

INTERFACING

Pellon Shape-Flex and Peltex
Ultra-Firm
pellonprojects.com

HeatnBond Fleece Fusible
thermowebonline.com

NOTIONS

Printed measuring tape/twill
tape
ribbonjar.com

KNITTING NEEDLES

Knit Picks
knitpicks.com

CONTRIBUTORS

Berene Campbell

Berene is a graphic designer who in recent years has spread her love of designing to fabric and sewing patterns. She has published patterns in books and is a regular contributor to *Stitch* magazine. A member of the Vancouver Modern Quilt Guild, Berene enjoys collaborating and connecting with the quilting community at large. She lives with her husband, two crafty kids, and their obstinate rabbit in North Vancouver, British Columbia, Canada. Find links to her blog, products, Etsy, and Spoonflower shops at happysewlucky.com.

Leanne Chahley

Leanne loves to play with color and fiber, so quilting is a perfect fit for her. When not quilting, Leanne has a busy professional career and a household filled with her young-adult children and her spouse's lovely music. She blogs at shecanquilt.blogspot.com.

Krista Fleckenstein

Krista lives and creates in Anchorage, Alaska, with her husband and four children. She grew up in a family of quilters, surrounded by fabric and the hum of a sewing machine. Today she continues her family's quilting traditions in her own way, focusing on improvisational design, screen-printing fabric, and pattern writing. Krista contributed to *Modern Quilts from the Blogging Universe* (Martingale, 2012) and blogs at spottedstone.blogspot.com.

Amy Friend

Amy left her career as a museum curator to raise her three children. From her home in West Newbury, Massachusetts, she now designs patterns. Her favorite patterns are foundation pieced. She was the founder and first president of the Seacoast Modern Quilt Guild. Amy's many patterns, free tutorials, and latest quilts can be found at duringquiettime.com.

Lynne Goldsworthy

Lynne is a modern British quilter who blogs at lilysquilts.blogspot.com. She's also a member of the editorial/design team of three quilters running the online quilting magazine *Fat Quarterly* (fatquarterly.com) and the annual London *Fat Quarterly* quilting retreats. She has contributed patterns to various books and magazines, coauthored a quilt-block book, as well as designed and made quilts for several fabric companies.

Christina Lane

Christina is a professional long-arm quilter and pattern designer residing in the beautiful Pacific Northwest. She's contributed to many publications over the years. Find out more about Christina at sometimescrafter.com.

Kristie Maslow

Kristie is a self-taught quilter and knitter who gets extended use out of her many cozy projects in wintery Winnipeg, Canada. She's a full-time mom to three kids and part-time dentist also. She's married to a very patient man trained to say, "I can't believe you made that!" She loves her family all the more when she's away on quilting retreats. You can learn more about Kristie and her projects on her blog, ocd-obsessivecraftingdisorder.blogspot.com.

Felicity Ronaghan

Felicity has been a quilter for nearly 15 years, but when she discovered the world of modern quilting online about four years ago, her passion went into overdrive. By day, she's a training and development consultant in the financial services industry; by night, she's a wife and mother who squeezes as much quilting as possible into every spare moment. She blogs about what she makes at www.felicityquilts.com.

Ayumi Takahashi

Ayumi lives in Tokyo with her husband from Seattle and her baby girl. Her projects have been featured in a book she authored as well as in magazines including *Stitch* and *Patchwork Tsushin*. Her favorite quilt is a lovely alphabet quilt that Krista Hennebury kindly put together for her baby with blocks made by bloggers from all over the world. For a wide range of beautiful *zakka* tutorials, visit Ayumi at ayumills.blogspot.com.

Cindy Wiens

Cindy comes from a rich heritage of quilting, stemming from her ancestors; an important part of that heritage includes being careful not to waste anything, including the selvages from the fabrics she uses in her quilts. Besides making quilts for family and friends, she regularly donates quilts to help raise money for disaster relief at an annual auction in her hometown of Fresno, California. Visit Cindy at liveacolorfullife.net.

Krista Withers

Krista lives and works in the beautiful, yet sometimes soggy, Pacific Northwest with her best friend and husband, Mike, and their two beautiful children. She is a professional long-arm machine quilter who has worked for the past seven years out of her garden studio behind their little house. Krista quilts on a Gammill Classic Plus endearingly known as the Tin Man, with the occasional assist of her beloved Intelliquilter, named Einstein. See what Krista's quilting next at kristawithersquilting.blogspot.com or check out her digital quilting designs (as seen on the "Orange Grove Quilt" on page 92) at digitechpatterns.com.

ACKNOWLEDGMENTS

Thank you Bryan, for working hard outside of our home so that I have the freedom to work hard within it. Your encouragement, support, and belief in my abilities hasn't wavered since the day we met in Hebb Theatre, and for that I'm so very grateful. Thanks for sleeping under the quilts I've made you, Tate and Devan, and for eating your fair share of frozen pizza. To the rest of my family, I truly appreciate your gracious acceptance of the handmade stuff I keep sending you for every occasion.

To the Gathered Threads, the Lions Gate Quilter's Guild, the Vancouver Modern Quilt Guild, and everyone who has enjoyed their days at Quilt by the Bay and their November weekend at Loon Lake: thanks for your friendship and enthusiastic support always! I love learning from, and sharing with, all of you.

The measurements for the traditional Pine Tree blocks (used in "Orange Grove Quilt" on page 92) were taken from Judy Hopkins' book *Five- and Seven-Patch Blocks & Quilts for the ScrapSaver™* (That Patchwork Place, 1992).

A huge heartfelt thanks to all of my lovely contributors who agreed to come on this virtual retreat with me by sharing their ideas and projects that fill the pages of this book. Thanks also to my local quilting pals who test drove "Rainbow 'Round the Cabin Quilt" (page 104) around my dining table.

To everyone at Martingale who helped me see this through from proposal, to project, to paper: I thank you for this opportunity!

~ Krista

ABOUT THE AUTHOR

KRISTA learned to sew in elementary school home-economics class where she made an outstanding drawstring book bag out of green-print corduroy and gold rope. Later, her Mom allowed Krista to use one of the first electronic Singer sewing machines to make a few sundresses, Halloween costumes, and hem her jeans. After years of dabbling in crafty sewing projects, she took a beginner quilting class at a local quilt shop in 2000 and instantly knew she had found her passion.

Now, after almost 14 years of taking workshops, teaching workshops, actively participating in both traditional and modern quilt guilds, and running a successful day-retreat business, Krista is thrilled to be a part of the exciting online blogging community. She makes traditionally informed modern-style quilts and a lot of bags. All of this magic happens in her small sewing-room-with-a-view near Vancouver, Canada, or on retreat with her sewing friends. Connect with Krista at poppyprintcreates.blogspot.com.

Photo by Luiza Matysiak

What's your creative passion?
Find it at **ShopMartingale.com**
books • eBooks • ePatterns • daily blog • free projects
videos • tutorials • inspiration • giveaways